FINDING YOUR BEARINGS

AUTHORS

Rosemarie Bezerra-Nader

Susan F. Lusk

Merriellen Cohrs

Scot Wahab

Julie Ann Davies

Doug Waltner

Susan B. Highlund

EDITOR

Ann Wiebe

ILLUSTRATORS

Brenda Dahl

Cheryl Long

AIMS is committed to remaining at the cutting edge of providing integrated studies that are user-friendly, educationally sound, developmentally appropriate, and aligned with the recommendations from national education documents.

Finding Your Bearings has been revised in order to maintain this high standard. The newly-formatted teacher's manual illustrates the alignment of our activities with the national documents, *Benchmarks for Science Literacy* (American Association for the Advancement of Science) and the *Curriculum and Evaluation Standards for School Mathematics* (National Council of Teachers of Mathematics). Where appropriate, suggestions are given for *open-ended* and/or *guided planning* procedures that challenge students to design their own plan for exploring a problem or question.

This book contains materials developed by the AIMS Education Foundation. **AIMS** (**A**ctivities Integrating **M**athematics and **S**cience) began in 1981 with a grant from the National Science Foundation. The non-profit AIMS Education Foundation publishes hands-on instructional materials (books and the monthly *AIMS* Magazine) that integrate curricular disciplines such as mathematics, science, language arts, and social studies. The Foundation sponsors a national program of professional development through which educators may gain both an understanding of the AIMS philosophy and expertise in teaching by integrated, hands-on methods.

ISBN **1-881431-45-2**

Printed in the United States of America

I HEAR AND I FORGET

I SEE AND I REMEMBER

I DO AND I UNDERSTAND

-Chinese Proverb

To The Teacher...

The earth does not seem as big as it used to be. Its physical size remains the same; it is the speed with which we can reach other countries that has changed. Links to most any place on the earth can be made instantly via satellite transmissions, fax machines, and computer telecommunication lines. Foreign countries are only a few hours away by jet. Since the world is truly our neighbor, we need citizens who are geographically literate.

Welcome to adventures in geography, adventures which integrate social science with math and science. Social science comes alive when taken out of textbooks and put into the hands of the students.

For too long, social science has been considered a read-and-answer-questions subject. We have all experienced the agony of memorizing lists of dates and facts. Social science takes on new meaning when combined with real world experiences and scientific discovery. The concepts become explorations that stimulate both creative and critical thought.

In addition to working with objects, your students will also have the chance to work with each other. They will practice essential social skills such as cooperating and compromising.

In *Finding Your Bearings*, students will have opportunities to discover, experience, and experiment with globes, road maps, relief maps, basketball courts, and shopping malls.

You may choose excursions through your room or journeys around the world. We wish you "bon voyage."

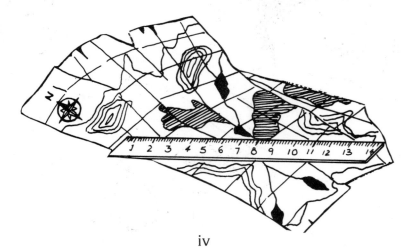

TABLE OF CONTENTS

SUPPLY LIST

This list may assist you in assembling the supplies for the activities you have chosen.

CONSUMABLE ITEMS

____ Colored pencils or crayons

____ Tag

____ Large white and colored construction paper

____ Graph paper, size optional

____ Cardboard for map bases

____ Paper fasteners

____ Large paper clips

____ Glue

____ Glue sticks

____ String

____ Newspaper weather reports

____ Two 1 lb. bags of lima beans

____ Masking tape

____ Flour, about 10 pounds

____ Salt, about 10 pounds

____ Gummed labels

____ Toothpicks

NON-CONSUMABLE ITEMS

____ Calculators

____ Protractors

____ Globes, as many as possible

____ 1 beachball globe

____ 5 or more U.S. road maps

____ Sample relief map

____ Scissors

____ Metric rulers

____ Meter sticks

____ Magnetic compasses

____ Drawing compasses

____ Resource books: almanacs, atlases, encyclopedias

____ Mixing containers

____ Measuring cups and spoons

____ Dinner knives

____ Rolling pins

GEOGRAPHY

LOCATION

Location can be described using
- hemispheres
- rectangular coordinates
- polar coordinates
- cardinal and intermediate directions
- the positions of countries relative to each other

REGIONS

Regions with common characteristics such as classrooms, shopping malls, and forested mountains can be represented by models and maps.

Regions change, sometimes over a long period of time.

MOVEMENT

Distances between places on maps and globes can be measured.

The highway system links places and influences the movement patterns of people.

HUMANS AND ENVIRONMENT

Physical features have a major effect on land use and the economy.

People adapt to the environment by choosing appropriate clothing.

PLACE

Areas of land and water, landforms and contours, and temperature patterns are physical characteristics of places.

Population growth patterns and density are human characteristics of places.

Places can be represented in a variety of ways and from different perspectives.

Project 2061 Benchmarks

Below you will find a listing of the *Benchmarks for Science Literacy* (American Association for the Advancement of Science) which are addressed in this publication.

- *Scientific knowledge is subject to modification as new information challenges prevailing theories and as a new theory leads to looking at old observations in a new way.*

- *Important contributions to the advancement of science, mathematics, and technology have been made by different kinds of people, in different cultures, at different times.*

- *Mathematics is the study of many kinds of patterns, including numbers and shapes and operations on them. Sometimes patterns are studied because they help to explain how the world works or how to solve practical problems, sometimes because they are interesting in themselves.*

- *The earth is mostly rock. Three-fourths of its surface is covered by a relatively thin layer of water (some of it frozen), and the entire planet is surrounded by a relatively thin blanket of air. It is the only body in the solar system that appears able to support life. The other planets have compositions and conditions very different from the earth's.*

- *In making decisions, it helps to take time to consider the benefits and drawbacks of alternatives.*

- *Trade between nations occurs when natural resources are unevenly distributed and the costs of production are very different in different countries. A nation has a trade opportunity whenever it can create more of a product or service at a lower cost than another.*

- *The global environment is affected by national policies and practices relating to energy use, waste disposal, ecological management, manufacturing, and population.*

- *Measurements are always likely to give slightly different numbers, even if what is being measured stays the same.*

- *Areas of irregular shapes can be found by dividing them into squares and triangles.*

- *Shapes on a sphere like the earth cannot be depicted on a flat surface without some distortion.*

- *The graphic display of numbers may help to show patterns such as trends, varying rates of change, gaps, or clusters. Such patterns sometimes can be used to make predictions about the phenomena being graphed.*

- *It takes two numbers to locate a point on a map or any other flat surface. The numbers may be two perpendicular distances from a point, or an angle and a distance from a point.*

- *Scale drawings show shapes and compare locations of things very different in size.*

- *The scale chosen for a graph or drawing makes a big difference in how useful it is.*

- *Probabilities are ratios and can be express-ed as fractions, percentages, or odds.*

- *The larger a well-chosen sample is, the more accurately it is likely to represent the whole, but there are many ways of choosing a sample that can make it unrepresentative of the whole.*

- *A small part of something may be special in some way and not give an accurate picture of the whole. How much a portion of something can help to estimate what the whole is like depends on how the portion is chosen. There is a danger of choosing only the data that show what is expected by the person doing the choosing.*

- *Events can be described in terms of being more or less likely, impossible, or certain.*

- *Sometimes people invent a general rule to explain how something works by summarizing observations. But people tend to overgeneralize, imagining general rules on the basis of only a few observations.*

- *Models are often used to think about processes that happen too slowly, too quickly, or on too small a scale to observe directly, or that are too vast to be changed deliberately, or that are potentially dangerous.*

- *Geometric figures, number sequences, graphs, diagrams, sketches, number lines, maps, and stories can be used to represent objects, events, and processes in the real world, although such representations can never be exact in every detail.*

- *Physical and biological systems tend to change until they become stable and then remain that way unless their surroundings change.*

Students should:

- *Offer reasons for their findings and consider reasons suggested by others.*

- *Estimate distances and travel times from maps and the actual size of objects from scale drawings.*

- *Measure and mix dry and liquid materials (in the kitchen, garage, or laboratory) in prescribed amounts, exercising reasonable safety.*

- *Organize information in simple tables and graphs and identify relationships they reveal.*

- *Locate information in reference books, back issues of newspapers and magazines, compact disks, and computer databases.*

- *Find and describe locations on maps with rectangular and polar coordinates.*

- *Use numerical data in describing and comparing objects and events.*

- *Seek better reasons for believing something than "Everybody knows that …" or "I just know" and discount such reasons when given by others.*

- *Be skeptical of arguments based on very small samples of data, biased samples, or samples for which there was no control sample.*

NCTM Standards

Below you will find a listing of the *Curriculum and Evaluation Standards for School Mathematics* (National Council of Teachers of Mathematics) which are addressed in this publication.

The mathematics curriculum should include numerous and varied experiences with problem solving as a method of inquiry and application so that students can–

- *Verify and interpret results with respect to the original problem situation*

Reasoning shall permeate the mathematics curriculum so that students can–

- *Recognize and apply deductive and inductive reasoning*

- *Understand and apply reasoning processes, with special attention to spatial reasoning and reasoning with proportions and graphs*

The mathematics curriculum should include the investigation of mathematical connections so that students can–

- *Use mathematics in other curriculum areas*

- *Explore problems and describe results using graphical, numerical, physical, algebraic, and verbal mathematical models or representations*

The mathematics curriculum should include the continued development of number and number relationships so that students can–

- *Understand and apply ratios, proportions, and percents in a wide variety of situations*

The mathematics curriculum should develop the concepts underlying computation and estimation in various contexts so that students can–

- *Compute with whole numbers, fractions, decimals, integers, and rational numbers*

- *Select and use an appropriate method for computing from among mental arithmetic, paper-and-pencil, calculator, and computer methods*

- *Use computation, estimation, and proportions to solve problems*

The mathematics curriculum should include explorations of patterns and functions so that students can–

- *Describe, extend, analyze, and create a wide variety of patterns*

The mathematics curriculum should include exploration of statistics in real-world situations so that students can–

- *Systematically collect, organize, and describe data*

- *Construct, read, and interpret tables, charts and graph*

- *Make inferences and convincing arguments that are based on data analysis*

The mathematics curriculum should include explorations of probability in real-world situations so that students can–

- *Model situations by devising and carrying out experiments or simulations to determine probabilities*

The mathematics curriculum should include the study of the geometry of one, two, and three dimensions in a variety of situations so that students can–

- *Visualize and represent geometric figures with special attention to developing spatial sense*

- *Develop an appreciation of geometry as a means of describing the physical world*

The mathematics curriculum should include extensive concrete experiences using measurement so that students can–

- *Estimate, make, and use measurements to describe and compare phenomena*

- *Select appropriate units and tools to measure to the degree of accuracy required in a particular situation*

- *Extend their understanding of the concepts of perimeter, area, volume, angle measure, capacity, and weight and mass*

- *Make and use estimates of measurement*

- *Make and use measurements in problems and everyday situations*

PROCESSES

	Predicting	Observing	Classifying	Collecting/recording data	Comparing	Identifying/controlling variables	Interpreting data	Inferring	Generalizing	Applying	Working cooperatively	Communicating ideas	Making/reading maps	Formulating questions	Considering multiple points of view	Appreciating rights/responsibilities
Surf 'n Sand Count	X	X	X	X	X				X		X	X	X			
Surf 'n Sand Spin	X	X	X	X	X				X		X	X	X			
Surf 'n Sand Toss		X	X	X	X				X		X	X	X			
Global AdVENNtures	X	X	X	X	X				X		X	X	X			
Drifting Apart		X			X			X			X	X				
Plot Your Position	X	X					X						X			
Physically Featured		X			X		X		X				X			
Economically Speaking		X	X		X		X	X	X		X	X	X			
I've Got the World on a String		X		X	X		X	X	X		X	X	X			
South American Jigsaw		X			X		X				X	X	X			
A Patch of North America		X			X		X				X	X	X			
Getting There		X		X	X						X	X	X	X		
Fire on the Mountain		X		X	X	X	X		X	X	X	X	X		X	
Forecast for Today	X	X		X	X		X	X	X	X						
Count Me In!		X		X	X	X	X	X	X		X	X				
People 'Plosion I	X	X			X		X	X			X	X	X		X	X
People 'Plosion II	X	X		X	X		X	X			X	X		X	X	X
Tic-Tac-Room		X		X	X						X	X	X			
Scale the Room		X		X	X		X				X	X	X			
Room to Move		X		X	X	X	X			X	X	X	X		X	
Shrinking Boundaries	X	X		X	X		X				X	X	X			
Bird's Eye View		X		X	X	X					X	X	X		X	
Shop 'Til You Drop		X		X	X		X				X	X	X		X	
Navigating Numerically		X		X	X		X	X	X		X	X	X			
Rallying Around	X	X		X	X		X				X	X	X			
What a Relief!		X			X		X				X	X	X			
Mystery Mountain		X	X		X		X				X	X	X	X		

MATH

	Estimation	Count	Measurement	Whole number operations	Formulas	Ratio and proportion	Decimals	Percent	Order	Patterns	Geometry and spatial sense	Statistics	Probability	Problem solving	Logic	Coordinates	Venn diagrams	Graphs
Surf 'n Sand Count	X	X		X		X	X	X										X
Surf 'n Sand Spin	X			X		X	X	X					X			X		X
Surf 'n Sand Toss		X		X		X	X	X					X					X
Global AdVENNtures																	X	
Drifting Apart														X				
Plot Your Position	X															X		
Physically Featured	X															X		
Economically Speaking	X		X	X		X	X	X										X
I've Got the World on a String	X		X	X		X	X											
South American Jigsaw														X	X			
A Patch of North America														X	X			
Getting There			X	X		X	X											
Fire on the Mountain	X		X	X										X				
Forecast for Today			X									X						X
Count Me In!		X	X	X	X							X						
People 'Plosion I	X		X							X		X						X
People 'Plosion II	X			X	X			X				X						X
Tic-Tac-Room	X		X													X		
Scale the Room	X		X	X		X												
Room to Move	X		X	X		X								X				
Shrinking Boundaries	X		X	X		X	X											
Bird's Eye View											X							
Shop 'Til You Drop			X	X		X					X							
Navigating Numerically										X					X	X		
Rallying Around	X		X	X	X	X	X											
What a Relief!			X															
Mystery Mountain			X			X				X	X							

Surf 'n Sand

This investigation deals with finding the ratio of water to land on the earth's surface via any one of the three activities. In *Surf 'n Sand Count*, squares of land and water are counted on a world map. In *Surf 'n Sand Spin*, latitude and longitude readings are generated by spinners and the land or water location found on a world map. In *Surf 'n Sand Toss*, an inflatable globe is tossed and a record made of land or water under the right index finger of the catcher. The circle graph can be used to summarize any of the activities. The continents and oceans sheet may be used as an extension for the *Spin* and *Toss* versions. Choose the activity best suited to your needs or have different groups do the various activities simultaneously, and compare their results.

Surf 'n Sand Count

Topic
Land/water area on earth

Key Question
How do the surface areas of land and water on the earth compare?

Focus
Students will discover the ratio of water to land on the earth's surface by estimating land or water areas within a square grid on a world map.

Math
NCTM Standards
- *Understand and apply ratios, proportions, and percents in a wide variety of situations*
- *Select and use an appropriate method for computing from among mental arithmetic, paper-and-pencil, calculator, and computer methods*
- *Systematically collect, organize, and describe data*

Estimation
   area
   rounding
Count
Whole number operations
Ratios
Decimals
Percent
Graphs

Project 2061 Benchmarks
- *Shapes on a sphere like the earth cannot be depicted on a flat surface without some distortion.*
- *The earth is mostly rock. Three-fourths of its surface is covered by a relatively thin layer of water (some of it frozen), and the entire planet is surrounded by a relatively thin blanket of air. It is the only body in the solar system that appears able to support life. The other planets have compositions and conditions very different from the earth's.*

- *Areas of irregular shapes can be found by dividing them into squares and triangles.*

Social Science
Geography
   world

Science
Earth science

Processes
Predicting
Observing
Classifying
Collecting and recording data
Comparing
Generalizing
Working cooperatively
Communicating ideas
Reading maps

Materials
Activity sheets: *Surf 'n Sand Count, Surf 'n Sand Circle Graph*
Calculators
Protractors
Colored pencils or crayons
Optional: transparencies of map and circle graph

Background Information
The earth's surface is about 71% water and 29% land. See *Land and Water on the Earth*.

A *Cylindrical Equal Space Projection* is used here, flattening the earth and putting it on an equally-spaced grid. The land masses near tne polar areas appear distorted in this type of projection.

When rounding squares that are more than 50% land or water, there will be approximately 60 squares of land and 180 squares of water. When visually estimating the squares the land would cover if compactly joined together in each column, there will be approximately 69 squares of land and 171 squares of water. Using the latter figures, land covers about 29% of the earth and water 71%. Your results may vary due to differences in estimating, but the total number of squares should be 240, the area of the 10 x 24 map grid. Even though using such a broad form of estimation, the results are fairly close to the real statistics. If the map grid squares were smaller, the results would be even more accurate.

Management

1. Teams of two will need about 60 minutes to complete the activity.
2. If land (or water) is estimated to cover half or more of any square on the grid, it should be counted as one land (or water) square. There is room for disagreement in some columns where the estimation is close, a good point for discussion. The final results will still be very similar. Land masses in a particular column may also be visually estimated according to how many squares they would take up if they were compactly joined together.
3. Consider making transparencies of the map and circle graph, as well as transparent protractors.

Procedure

1. Have students predict and record the percent of water on the earth's surface.
2. Students should count and record the number of land squares and the number of water squares in each column. Totals should always equal ten. *Optional view* – Turn the paper sideways and count the long columns.
3. Have students find the total land squares and total water squares for the entire map.
4. Direct students to find the total area of the map grid and figure the percent of land and water using the table below the map.
5. Lead a discussion comparing class results. The columns are labeled with letters for easy reference. Differences of opinion may not always be resolved; allow any legitimate estimations. A map transparency is helpful.
6. Students should complete the computation on the top of the circle graph page, construct and label the graph, and summarize their data in written form. Use a circle graph transparency and transparent protractor to help less experienced students get started. An example of the computation:

    360 x .29 (land) = 104 degrees
    360 x .71 (water) = 256 degrees
7. Discuss additional questions.

Discussion

1. What percent of the earth's surface is water? [about 71%] How does this compare with your prediction?
2. Were all results exactly the same? [probably not] Why not? [differences in estimation of area within a square; some squares can be argued for either land or water]
3. A graph title should tell others, in brief form, what the graph represents. What title did you pick? [Surface Area of the Earth, etc.] Does it contain too much information? ...Too little?
4. We have expressed the results in decimals and percents. What other number forms could be used? [ratio: 7:3 water to land; fraction: 7/10 water and 3/10 land]

Extensions

1. Compare the area of the four major oceans using the same map grid. Make a table and rank them from largest to smallest.
2. Use the map grid to compare the area of the seven continents and rank them from largest to smallest. Draw the boundary between Europe and Asia.

Curriculum Correlation

Language Arts

1. Brainstorm words describing water (liquid, blue, splash, float, molecules, pour...) and land (solid, mud, rock, cracks, molecules, brown...) Are there any words which describe both water and land? Make a Venn diagram with the words that have been collected.
2. Prepare an advertisement which will attract creatures from other planets to vacation on the earth based on the fact that it is largely water.

Math

To further explore the area of irregular shapes, see *Area the Easy Way* in Vol. VIII, No. 2 of the *AIMS* magazine.

Art

Color graph paper squares in a ratio of 7 to 3 (like the ratio of water to land) using two colors. The designs could be symmetrical.

2

Surf 'n Sand Spin

Topic
Land/water area on earth

Key Question
How do the surface areas of land and water on the earth compare?

Focus
Students will discover the ratio of water to land on the earth's surface by using spinners to randomly select latitude and longitude and finding the land or water location on a world map.

Math
NCTM Standards
- *Understand and apply ratios, proportions, and percents in a wide variety of situations*
- *Systematically collect, organize, and describe data*
- *Model situations by devising and carrying out experiments or simulations to determine probabilities*

Estimation
    rounding
Whole number operations
Ratios
Decimals
Percent
Probability
Coordinates
Graphs

Project 2061 Benchmarks
- *The earth is mostly rock. Three-fourths of its surface is covered by a relatively thin layer of water (some of it frozen), and the entire planet is surrounded by a relatively thin blanket of air. It is the only body in the solar system that appears able to support life. The other planets have compositions and conditions very different from the earth's.*
- *Probabilities are ratios and can be expressed as fractions, percentages, or odds.*
- *The larger a well-chosen sample is, the more accurately it is likely to represent the whole, but there are many ways of choosing a sample that can make it unrepresentative of the whole.*
- *Find and describe locations on maps with rectangular and polar coordinates.*

Social Science
Geography
    world

Science
Earth science

Processes
Predicting
Observing
Classifying
Collecting and recording data
Comparing
Generalizing
Working cooperatively
Communicating ideas
Reading maps

Materials
For the class:
    activity sheets: *Surf 'n Sand Spin, Surf 'n Sand Circle Graph*
    protractors
    colored pencils or crayons
    optional: transparency of circle graph
For each group:
    1 manila folder or piece of tag
    2 large paper fasteners
    2 large paper clips
    at least 1 globe or world map with latitude and longitude

Background Information
The earth is about 71% water and 29% land. The use of spinners to determine random latitude and longitude readings results in a probability experiment that, if repeated many times, should yield numbers fairly close to the actual percentages. The more trials, the greater the accuracy. See *Land and Water on the Earth*.

Management
1. Groups of four are recommended – a spinner, two map readers, and a recorder. It is important to double-check latitude/longitude locations. Each map reader should have their own map (from history texts, atlases, etc.); encourage the use of different kinds within the group.
2. The activity is set up for two sets of ten trials. If locating latitude and longitude is a difficult skill, one set of ten trials may be used per group. However, more trials yield greater accuracy in the final results.
3. Before beginning the activity, prepare the spinners according to the directions. If you use the top of a manila folder for the spinners, the group's papers can be stored inside.
4. Decide whether students should estimate the spin reading to the nearest five degrees or to the nearest degree.

Procedure

1. Have students predict and record the percent of water on the earth's surface.
2. Students should spin both spinners, then estimate and record the latitude/longitude readings with hemisphere abbreviations (Example: 45° N, 30° W).
3. Instruct students to find the latitude/longitude location on a map and record whether it is on land or in water.
4. Have students figure the land and water totals.
5. Guide the reporting of group totals to the class. Students should record these in Class Results and find the grand total. Then they should add the grand totals to get the total number of spins.
6. Direct students to find the percent of land and water using the table at the bottom of the sheet. The ratio is written as the land total over total spins and the water total over total spins.
7. Students should complete the computation on the top of the circle graph page, construct and label the graph, and summarize their data in written form. Use a circle graph transparency and transparent protractor to help less experienced students get started. An example of the computation:

    360 x .29 (land) = 104 degrees
    360 x .71 (water) = 256 degrees

8. Discuss additional questions.

Discussion

1. What percent of the earth's surface is water? [about 71%] How does this compare with your prediction?
2. How close were our results to the actual facts? What factors might cause differences? [spinners not constructed to move freely or without bias and, therefore, not truly random; errors in map reading; not enough trials; etc.]
3. A graph title should tell others, in brief form, what the graph represents. What title did you pick [Surface Area of the Earth, etc.] Does it contain too much information? ...Too little?
4. We have expressed the results in decimals and percents. What other number forms could be used? [ratio: 7:3 water to land; fraction: 7/10 water and 3/10 land]

Extension

Use *Surf 'n Sand Oceans and Continents* to compare ocean and continent areas. Calculate and graph each ocean and continent percentage.

Curriculum Correlation

See *Surf 'n Sand Count* for suggestions.

Surf 'n Sand Toss

Topic
Land/water area on earth

Key Question
If an inflatable globe is tossed and caught, what percent of the time will the catcher's right index finger be on water?

Focus
Students will discover the ratio of water to land on the earth's surface by tossing an inflatable globe and recording whether the right index finger touches land or water.

Math
NCTM Standards
- *Understand and apply ratios, proportions, and percents in a wide variety of situations*
- *Systematically collect, organize, and describe data*
- *Model situations by devising and carrying out experiments or simulations to determine probabilities*

Count
Whole number operations
Ratios
Decimals
Percent
Probability
Graphs

Project 2061 Benchmarks
- *The earth is mostly rock. Three-fourths of its surface is covered by a relatively thin layer of water (some of it frozen), and the entire planet is surrounded by a relatively thin blanket of air. It is the only body in the solar system that appears able to support life. The other planets have compositions and conditions very different from the earth's.*
- *Probabilities are ratios and can be expressed as fractions, percentages, or odds.*
- *The larger a well-chosen sample is, the more accurately it is likely to represent the whole, but there are many ways of choosing a sample that can make it unrepresentative of the whole.*

Social Science
Geography
    world

Science
Earth science

Processes
Observing
Classifying
Collecting and recording data
Comparing
Generalizing

4

Working cooperatively
Communicating ideas
Reading maps

Materials
Activity sheets: *Surf 'n Sand Toss, Surf 'n Sand Circle Graph*
Inflatable globe (available in toy stores)
Optional: transparency of circle graph

Background Information
The earth is covered by huge amounts of water. Over seventy percent of the earth's surface is water, leaving less than thirty percent for land. In this activity, the percentages will be calculated by doing a probability experiment in which a globe is repeatedly tossed and caught. The larger the number of tosses, the more closely the results should reflect the actual percentages. See *Land and Water on the Earth.*

Management
This activity can be done with the whole class. You may want to make some rules about how to toss and catch the globe. Spin the globe as it is tossed to insure randomness. Each student can make an individual tally as the globe is thrown or one person can make a tally on the board and the students can fill in the results after the three sets of trials are completed.

Procedure
1. Ask the *Key Question.*
2. Discuss the rules for tossing and catching the globe, and decide how the tallying will be done.
3. Have students toss and catch the ball 50 times and keep a tally in the space for Trial 1. They should record the ratio (land total over total spins and water total over total spins) and the percent in the percent table.
4. Repeat the process for Trials 2 and 3.
5. Students should find the average percent of land and water.
6. Students should complete the computation on the top of the circle graph page, construct and label the graph, and summarize their data in written form. Use a circle graph transparency and transparent protractor to help less experienced students get started. An example of the computation:
   360 x .29 (land) = 104 degrees
   360 x .71 (water) = 256 degrees
7. Discuss additional questions.

Discussion
1. What did you prove by doing this activity?
2. What factors could have affected the outcome? [doing a small number of tosses, someone's finger moving after catching the globe, not spinning the globe during the toss, etc.]
3. If you were to get one toss and catch, where would you predict your finger would land? [The chances are greater you would be touching water.]

Extension
Use *Surf 'n Sand Oceans and Continents* to keep track of the ocean or continent on which your finger lands. Calculate and graph each ocean and continent percentage.

Curriculum Correlation
See *Surf 'n Sand Count* for suggestions.

Surf 'n Sand Count

~ ~ ~ PREDICT WHAT PERCENT OF THE EARTH'S SURFACE IS WATER. _____ (0-100)

Names _____

Count the number of squares of land and water in each column.

CYLINDRICAL EQUAL SPACE PROJECTION

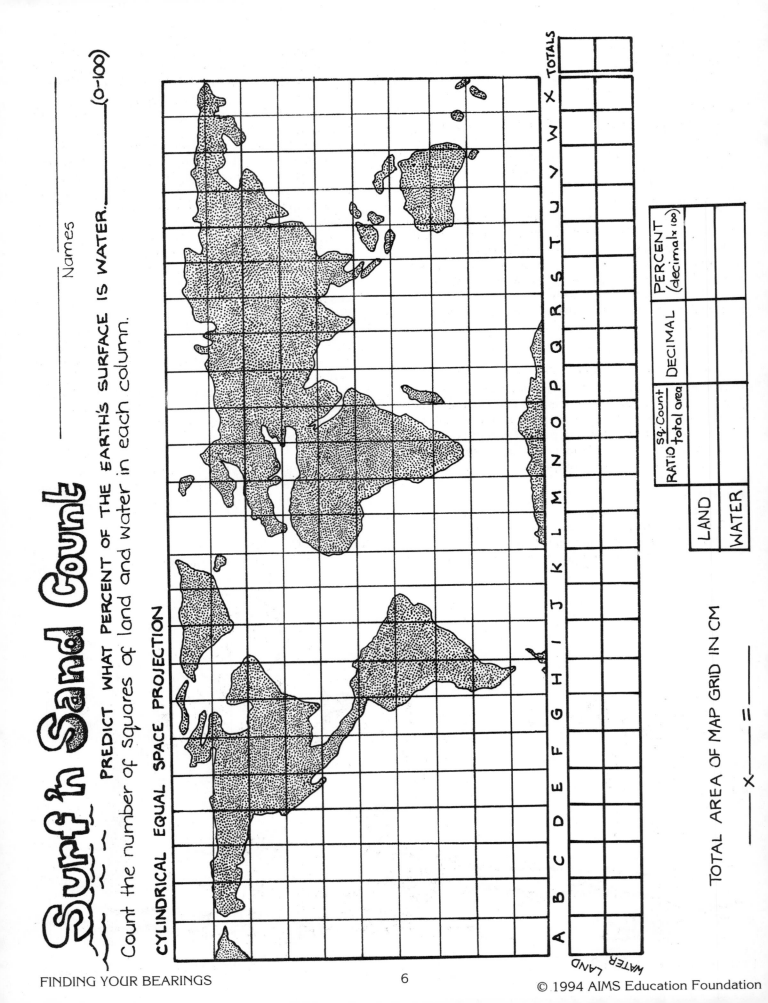

	A	B	C	D	E	F	G	H	I	J	K	L	M	N	O	P	Q	R	S	T	U	V	W	X	TOTALS
LAND																									
WATER																									

	RATIO Sq. Count / total area	DECIMAL	PERCENT (decimal x 100)
LAND			
WATER			

TOTAL AREA OF MAP GRID IN CM

____ x ____ =

Surf 'n Sand Spin

_____

_____

_____
Names

Predict the percent of water on the earth's surface. _____ (0—100)

Spin for latitude and longitude. Record the degrees and locate on a map or globe. Complete the tables.

LAT.	LONG.	LAND(L) OR WATER(W)?

LAT.	LONG.	LAND(L) OR WATER(W)?

TOTAL # LAND _____

TOTAL # WATER _____

CLASS RESULTS

GROUP	A	B	C	D	E	F	G	H	I	J	GRAND TOTAL
# LAND											
# WATER											

TOTAL SPINS

	RATIO # counted / total spins	DECIMAL	PERCENT (decimal x 100)
LAND			
WATER			

Surf 'n' Sand Spin...

Mount on tag or a manila folder. Insert a paper fastener in each center with a large paper clip attached. Wrap a thin piece of tape around the tip of the paper clip and cut to make an arrow.

LONGITUDE

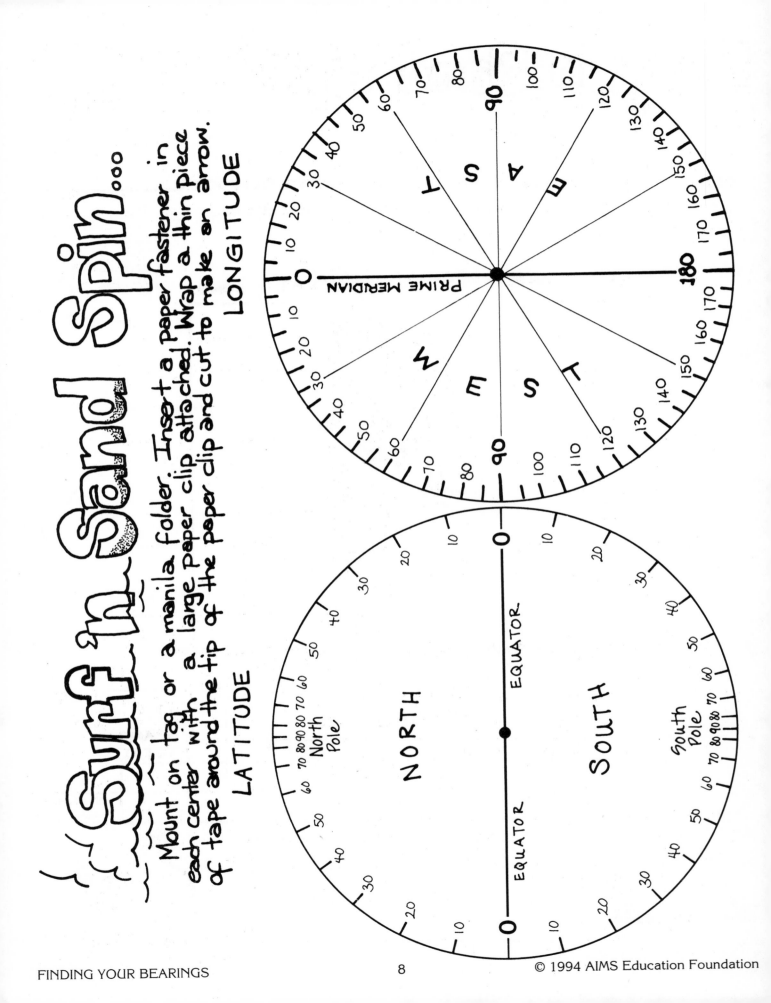

PRIME MERIDIAN

EAST

WEST

LATITUDE

North Pole

NORTH

EQUATOR

SOUTH

South Pole

Surf 'n Sand

Name _____

CIRCLE GRAPH

Total degrees in circle	Decimal	# of degrees representing area

_____ X _____ = _____
          land

_____ X _____ = _____
          water

Use a protractor to construct a circle graph showing your data. Label and color the graph. Give it a title.

_____
_____

Summarize your data: _____

_____

Name_____

Surf 'n Sand Toss

If an inflatable globe is tossed and caught, what percent of the time will the catcher's right index finger be on water?

Do three trials in which the globe is tossed and caught 50 times. Keep a tally of the results in the first table and then calculate the percents in the second table.

Tally

Trial	Land	Water
1		
2		
3		

Percents

Trial	Land/Total	Percent Land	Water/Total	Percent Water
1				
2				
3				
	Average		Average	

Surf 'n Sand

OCEANS AND CONTINENTS

How does the surface area of each ocean and continent compare?

Taking 100 spins or tosses, tally the number of times you land in each ocean or continent.

	TALLY	RATIO	%
ARCTIC			
ATLANTIC			
INDIAN			
PACIFIC			
AFRICA			
ANTARCTICA			
ASIA			
AUSTRALIA			
EUROPE			
NORTH AMERICA			
SOUTH AMERICA			
TOTAL			

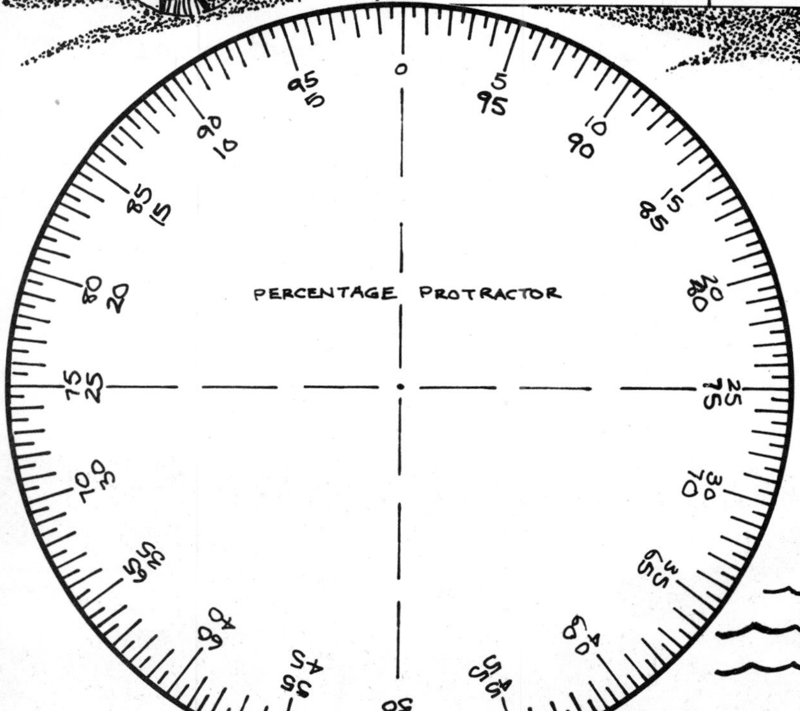

PERCENTAGE PROTRACTOR

Graph the percents. Label and color.

11

© 1994 AIMS Education Foundation

LAND AND WATER ON THE EARTH

The earth covers a surface of about 317,100,000 square kilometers (197,000,000 sq. miles). Approximately 71% of this surface is water and 29% is land. About 60% of the Northern Hemisphere is covered by water; in the Southern Hemisphere it is about 80%. The world's oceans have an average mean depth of 3,729 meters (12,234 ft.). The deepest place in the ocean is a V-shaped groove called the Mariana Trench (11,033m or 36,198ft.); it is located in the Pacific Ocean.

Though the earth's oceans are really part of one continuous body of water, geographers have defined the oceans' boundaries. The Pacific and Atlantic are divided by the meridian straight south from Cape Horn, the Atlantic and Indian by one south from the Cape of Good Hope, and the Indian and Pacific by one south from Australia and through Tasmania. The Arctic Ocean is bounded mostly by land around the Arctic Circle.

OCEAN	AREA in sq.km	(sq. miles)	% OF EARTH'S SURFACE
Pacific	112,700,000	(70,000,000)	35.5%
Atlantic	58,600,000	(36,400,000)	18.5%
Indian	46,000,000	(28,600,000)	14.5%
Arctic	7,600,000	(4,700,000)	2.4%
	224,900,000	(139,700,000)	70.9%

LAND AND WATER ON THE EARTH

The Northern Hemisphere contains more than two thirds of the earth's land surface. All of the continents except Antarctica are wider in the north than in the south, giving them a wedge-shaped appearance. Europe is the only continent without a more or less separate land mass; it is really a peninsula of Asia and sometimes these two continents together are called Eurasia.

CONTINENT	AREA in sq. km	(sq. miles)	% OF EARTH'S SURFACE
Asia	27,500,000	(17,100,000)	8.7%
Africa	19,000,000	(11,800,000)	6.0%
North America	13,700,000	(8,500,000)	4.3%
South America	11,100,000	(6,900,000)	3.5%
Antarctica	9,700,000	(6,000,000)	3.1%
Europe	6,400,000	(4,000,000)	2.0%
Australia	4,800,000	(3,000,000)	1.5%
	92,200,000	(57,300,000)	29.1%

Global AdVENNtures

Topic
Hemispheres/continents and oceans

Key Question
Which continents and/or oceans touch all four hemispheres?

Focus
Students will determine the hemispheric locations of the seven continents and four major oceans and use a Venn diagram to illustrate their findings.

Math
NCTM Standards
- *Systematically collect, organize, and describe data*
- *Construct, read, and interpret tables, charts and graphs*

Venn diagrams

Project 2061 Benchmarks
- *Find and describe locations on maps with rectangular and polar coordinates.*
- *Organize information in simple tables and graphs and identify relationships they reveal.*

Social Science
Geography
world

Processes
Predicting
Observing
Classifying
Collecting and recording data
Comparing
Generalizing
Working cooperatively
Communicating ideas
Reading maps

Materials
Globes or world maps with latitude/longitude lines

Background Information
According to *Webster's New World Dictionary*, a continent is "any of the main large land areas of the earth,

conventionally regarded with or without outlying islands...." A choice must be made whether to include or exclude outlying islands; both options are valid. The interpretation used particularly affects the northern/southern hemispheric classification of Asia. The answer keys shown here exclude outlying islands, such as Indonesia, though they would be considered a part of the continent culturally.

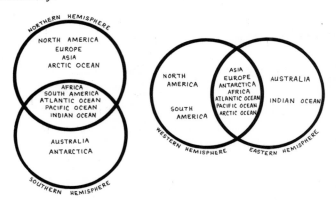

Venn diagrams are one form of logical thinking. They are a useful way to compare and contrast two or more attributes. In this activity, the attributes are the world's four hemispheres: northern, southern, eastern, and western. The two-circle Venn is used to compare two hemispheres, the four-circle Venn for all four hemispheres.

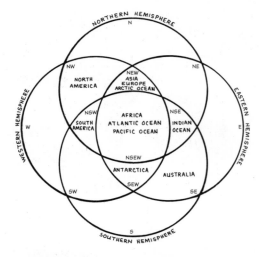

The *Goode's Equal Area Projection*, one of the maps included in the atlas, is a special map which is drawn on a flat surface but illustrates that the earth is round. The equator divides the earth into Northern and Southern Hemispheres, while the prime meridian (0 degrees longitude) and the international date line (mostly at 180 degrees longitude) divide the earth into Eastern and Western Hemispheres. The prime meridian runs through the original site of the Royal Observatory in Greenwich, England, a few kilometers from London. The international date line, on the opposite side of the world, is the place where each calendar day begins.

Management

1. Globes are preferable to maps. Borrow enough so that each group has one. Otherwise, use one of the maps at the end of this book.
2. Groups of two to four are suggested. Data can be recorded on one group sheet or by each group member individually.
3. Acquaint students with terms such as hemisphere, longitude, latitude, equator, and prime meridian prior to doing this activity.
4. Decide which Venn diagram is appropriate for the class: two circles comparing the Northern/Southern or Eastern/Western Hemispheres or four circles comparing all the hemispheres.
5. It is helpful for students to organize data for the four-circle Venn in a table with the following headings: NW, NEW, NE, NSE, SE, SEW, SW, NSW, and NSEW. Label the Venn the same way.
6. On the four-circle Venn, colored pencils can be used to shade the two-hemisphere intersections one color, the three-hemisphere intersections another color, etc.
7. Allow two or more 45-minute periods.
8. Transparencies are helpful to guide students inexperienced with Venn diagrams.

(Following are two different approaches for presenting this lesson in addition to the usual *Procedure.* These are offered for those teachers whose students are prepared for more independent investigations.)

Open-ended: Ask the *Key Question* and have student groups devise their own plan for collecting the data and showing the results.

Guided Planning: Organize students into planning groups. Then ask the *Key Question,* followed by these questions:

1. What do we need to know to begin our planning? [names of the hemispheres and how they are related, number of continents and oceans (to later check for completeness)]
2. What is your prediction?
3. How are you going to collect and organize your information?
4. How will you show the results?
5. What supplies are needed?
6. What are the responsibilities of each group member?

Procedure

1. Ask the Key Question and have students predict the answer without using a map. "None" is a possible prediction.
2. Have student groups use a globe or world map to complete the activity sheet. If using the map in this book, students should label the continents, oceans, equator, and prime meridian first. Group roles may be assigned or students can take turns classifying the continents and oceans.
3. If the *Goode's Projection* is used, explain its purpose.
4. On the second day, have students label and complete a Venn diagram.
5. Lead a class discussion.

Discussion

1. What continents and/or oceans are in all four hemispheres? [Africa, Atlantic Ocean, Pacific Ocean]
2. What line divides the Northern and Southern Hemispheres? [equator] Where is it located? [0° latitude]
3. What lines divide the Eastern and Western Hemispheres? [prime meridian, international date line] Where are they located? [0° longitude, 180° longitude]
4. On the four-circle Venn diagram, why are there no listings on the outside or non-intersecting spaces? [Every continent and ocean has a north/south location as well as an east/west location.]
5. Comparing Northern/Southern and then Eastern/Western, which hemispheres appear to have the most land? [Northern, Eastern] ...most water? [Southern, Western]
6. What are some examples of two ideas or events that can be compared by organizing them into a Venn diagram? [the views of two presidential candidates, the positive points of two prospective universities, etc.]

Extensions

1. There is no listing for the south/west intersection in the four-circle Venn. Challenge students to find some islands which would qualify for that intersection [South Sandwich Islands, Falkland Island in the Atlantic Ocean, Pitcairn Island, Tahiti, Cook Island in the Pacific Ocean, etc.]
2. Find islands for the north/east intersection as above.
3. Use Venn diagrams to show the interests or hobbies of four friends.
4. Do other Venn activities such as *Can You Planet?* from the AIMS book, *Out of This World.*

Curriculum Correlation

Language Arts

Have students use a Venn diagram to organize their thoughts or research when comparing and contrasting two concepts, two literary characters, etc.

Global AdVENNtures

1. Predict by circling the continents and/or oceans which touch all four hemispheres:

NORTH AMERICA   SOUTH AMERICA   EUROPE   ASIA   AFRICA   AUSTRALIA   ANTARCTICA

PACIFIC OCEAN   ATLANTIC OCEAN   ARCTIC OCEAN   INDIAN OCEAN

2. Use a globe or map to classify the continents and oceans listed above according to their locations in the Northern and Southern Hemispheres.

NORTHERN HEMISPHERE ONLY	BOTH HEMISPHERES	SOUTHERN HEMISPHERE ONLY

3. Classify the continents and oceans by Eastern and Western Hemispheres.

WESTERN HEMISPHERE ONLY	BOTH HEMISPHERES	EASTERN HEMISPHERE ONLY

4. Which continents and/or oceans touch all four hemispheres?

16

Global AdVENNtures

LABEL THE
HEMISPHERES.

17

Global AdVENNtures

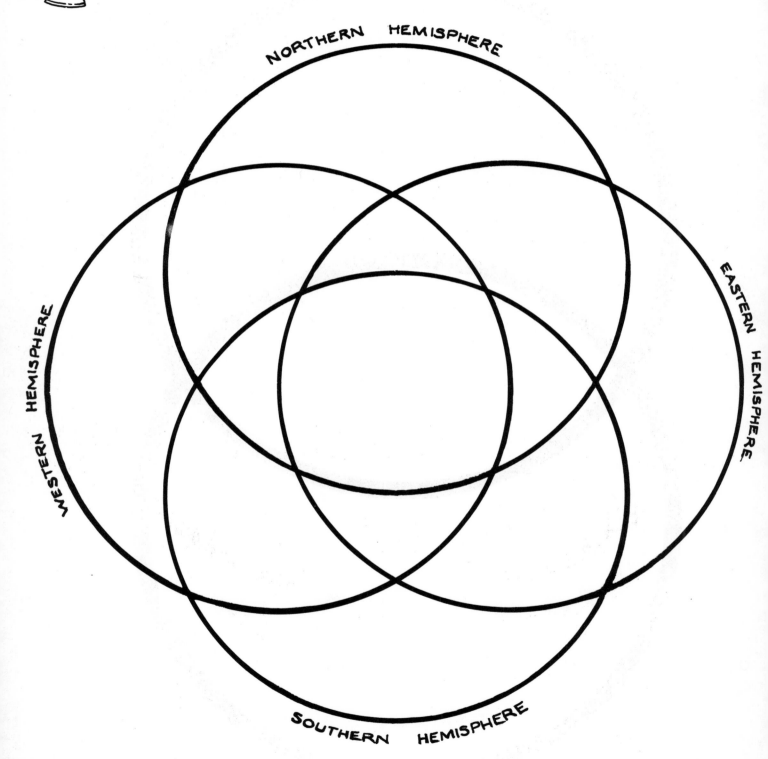

NORTHERN HEMISPHERE

WESTERN HEMISPHERE

EASTERN HEMISPHERE

SOUTHERN HEMISPHERE

DRIFTING APART

Topic
Continental drift theory

Key Question
How might the land on earth have once been joined together as one supercontinent?

Focus
Students will use a jigsaw puzzle format to determine how the continents may have once fit together.

Math
NCTM Standards
- *Recognize and apply deductive and inductive reasoning*
- *Understand and apply reasoning processes, with special attention to spatial reasoning and reasoning with proportions and graphs*

Problem solving

Project 2061 Benchmarks
- *Scientific knowledge is subject to modification as new information challenges prevailing theories and as a new theory leads to looking at old observations in a new way.*
- *Important contributions to the advancement of science, mathematics, and technology have been made by different kinds of people, in different cultures, at different times.*
- *Shapes on a sphere like the earth cannot be depicted on a flat surface without some distortion.*
- *Events can be described in terms of being more or less likely, impossible, or certain.*

Social Science
History/geography
  world

Science
Earth science
  geology

Processes
Observing
Comparing
Inferring
Working cooperatively
Communicating ideas

Materials
Scissors

Optional:
  scraps of cloth or unbleached muslin
    (about 30cm x 43 cm or 12" x 17")
  transparency of activity sheet
  blank paper
  glue

Background Information
See *Continental Drift Theory*. When first introduced in 1912, it was rejected. Since the 1960's, accumulating evidence and new explanations of why it might have happened have won over many scientists. However, it is still a theory. The significance of this theory is that it helps us 1) understand earthquakes and volcanoes and 2) understand the way mineral resources are distributed.

The possible joining of the continents would have happened along the edges of the continental shelves, not the shorelines. The shorelines have changed due to variable water levels and the growth of new formations over millions of years. Maps of the continental shelves are not common so the standard continental shapes have been taken from a globe and generalized for this activity. Therefore, the fit will not be as close.

The actual continent-to-continent fit that may have made up the supercontinent, Pangaea, is described in *Procedure*. *A word of caution:* The evidence most strongly supports the position of South America adjoining western Africa. The other continental positions do not have as much documentation and, therefore, maps in various sources may differ somewhat. One version is included in the fact sheet. Millions of years ago, India was separate from Asia and is represented that way on the activity sheet.

Management
1. Partners are recommended for this activity.
2. A transparency of the land masses, cut apart, can help illustrate their position in Pangaea.
3. Because the earth is spherical, it is impossible to give an accurate representation of the continents on a flat surface. To minimize this distortion, the land masses on a globe can be traced onto cloth by students and used to reconstruct Pangaea.

Procedure
1. Ask the *Key Question*.
2. Have students label and cut out the land masses on the activity sheet. Using a world map, they should draw a compass rose on each piece to compare the present orientation with the positions when Pangaea may have existed.

19

3. Give students a specified amount of time, five to ten minutes, to explore how the supercontinent may have fit together.
4. Students should follow teacher directions for placing the land masses in the positions suggested by the continental drift theory. Transparent land mass pieces may be used on the overhead for visual assistance.

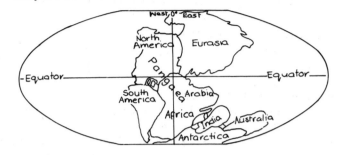

Directions for Pangaea
a. Place the eastern edge of South America against the lower western half of Africa.
b. Move the eastern coast of North America so that it touches the northwestern side of Africa.
c. Set southern Eurasia so that it joins North America and northern Africa. (The exact position varies with the source.)
d. Sandwich Greenland between North America and Eurasia.
e. Position western India against eastern Africa.
f. Place western Australia next to eastern India.
g. Connect eastern Antarctica with southern Australia.
h. Join Antarctica with southern Africa.

5. Glue the pieces in place on another sheet of paper (optional).
6. Review the information on the fact sheet and discuss the questions.

Discussion
1. Do you think Pangaea once existed? Why or why not?
2. In which direction is each of the continents moving?

Extensions
1. Study a map of the ocean floors. Trace the mid-ocean ridge and the connecting mountains as they wind continuously through the world. Notice that all the ocean waters are joined.
2. Compare maps of the earthquake areas, volcanic belts, and the earth's plates. How are they related? Write **The National Science Teachers Association, 1742 Connecticut Avenue, N.W., Washington, DC 20009** for the NSTA/FEMA publication of K-6 activities, *Earthquakes*, ISBN 0-87355-082-X.
3. Based on the movement of the continents, make predictions of how the earth will look 300 million years from now.

Curriculum Correlation
Language Arts
1. Write a biography of Wegener and trace the developments leading to his theory of continental drift.
2. Research the developments in the 1960's which led to the idea of plate tectonics. Pretend you are a reporter for *Scientific American*; write an article explaining the *who, what, when, where,* and *why* of these developments.

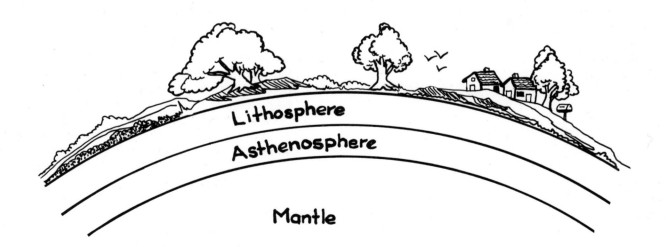

DRIFTING APART

Finish labeling these major land masses and cut them out. Mark North on each piece.

How might these pieces have fit together as one supercontinent?

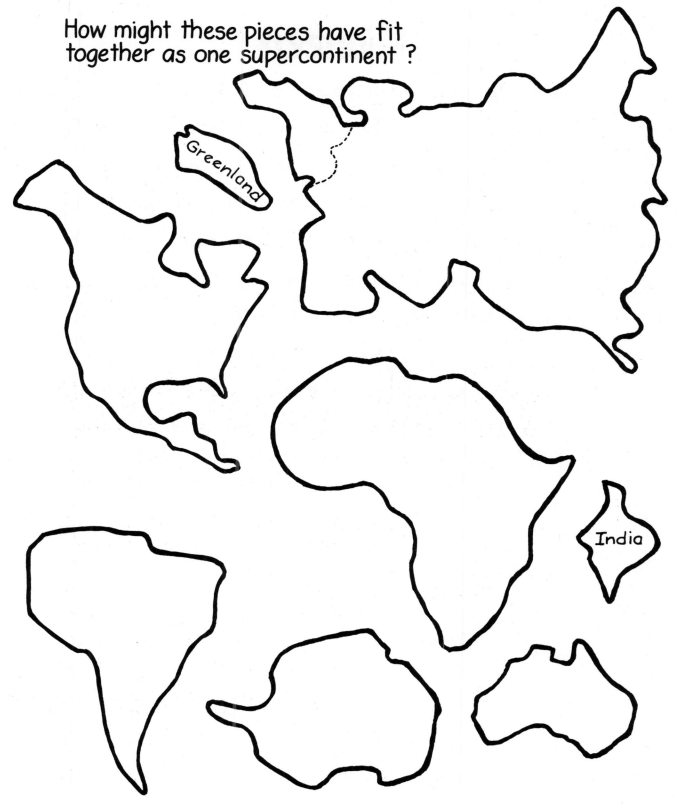

Continental Drift Theory
A Pioneer

In 1912 the German meteorologist and explorer, Alfred Wegener, presented the theory that the continents were once joined together in one big land mass and have, over millions of years, slowly drifted apart into their present positions. He named this supercontinent Pangaea, a Greek word meaning "all land." The rest of the earth's surface was covered with a massive ocean called Panthalassa. Over time, Pangaea split into two subcontinents. Laurasia in the north contained present-day Asia, Europe, and North America. Gondwanaland in the south included South America, Africa, India (then separate from Asia), Australia, and Antarctica.

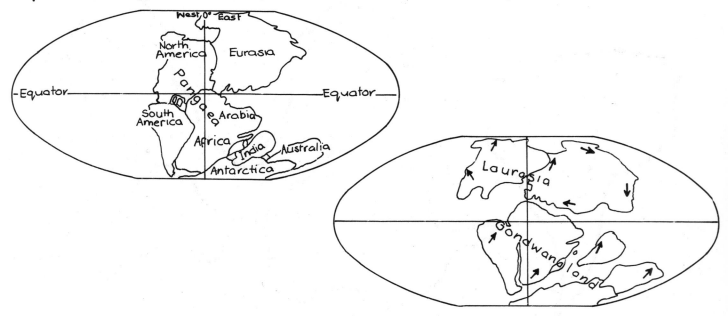

His theory was fiercely rejected at that time. What did a meteorologist, an outsider, know about geology? Since the 1960's, the theory has gained general acceptance among scientists.

Alfred Wegener was born in Berlin on Nov. 1, 1880. He studied astronomy and meteorology, receiving his doctorate in 1904. As a teacher, he inspired enthusiasm and strong loyalty. He authored a meteorology textbook which was used throughout Germany.

Wegener wondered, "Why should tropical ferns have grown in London, Paris, and even Greenland, yet glaciers have covered Brazil and the Congo at the same time?" He collected evidence from rocks, fossils, and the climate of the various continents to show they had once been joined together.

Ancient mountain systems, called cratons, show a connection between continents. Rocks in Africa and South America are of the same age and type; the diamond fields of South Africa and Brazil are an example. Supporting evidence also comes from the distribution of ancient and living organisms. Fossils of similar land animals have been found by paleontologists in the rocks of Asia, Europe, and North America. A change in the position of the continents would also explain why plants similar to those in tropical areas once grew in Greenland and glaciers once covered the equatorial regions of Africa and Brazil.

The Structure of the Earth

The earth has three layers: the crust, the mantle, and the core. The earth's crust is about 10 kilometers thick on the ocean floor and 32-72 kilometers thick on the continents, depending on elevation. The oldest rocks in the crust are about 3.8 billion years old, as measured by radiocarbon dating. The most predominant topographical feature of the earth's crust is the mid-ocean ridge, part of a 75,000 kilometer long mountain range that curls through all the oceans of the world like the seam on a baseball.

Sea Spreading

In the 1960's, sea spreading was advanced as an explanation for the movement of the land. It was shown that the ocean floor is spreading apart at the mid-ocean ridges, about one centimeter per year on each side of the ridge. Molten rock comes up through large cracks in the ocean ridges, cools, and slowly pushes the ocean floor and continents away from the ridges. The size of the earth is not changing, so if it is growing at the ridges, it must be shrinking somewhere else. Plate tectonics and convection currents offer a possible explanation.

Plate Tectonics

The crust and upper part of the mantle are called the lithosphere or rock sphere. Below it lies the asthenosphere, a soft, semisolid layer of rock which flows plastically due to high temperatures and tremendous pressures.

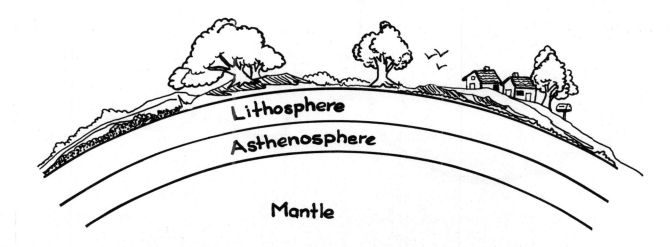

According to an explanation developed in 1968 called plate tectonics, the earth's crust is split into seven to twelve major plates and several smaller ones. These strong, rigid plates float on the asthenosphere. Most take their names from the continent, ocean, or area they cover. The plates move by spreading apart, sliding, or colliding. Earthquakes and volcanic eruptions take place along the edges of these plates. They move 2-15 centimeters a year, about the rate your fingernails grow.

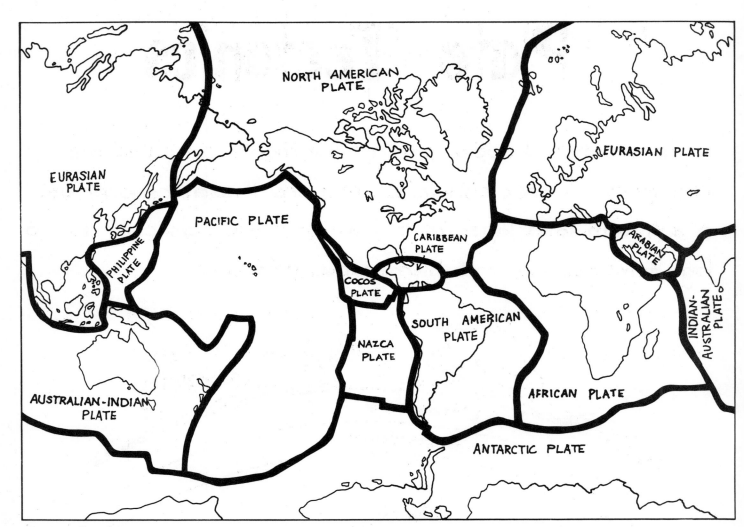

What drives the movement of the plates? Wegener thought it was centrifugal force caused by the earth's rotation. Scientists now favor convection currents, systems of heat exchange, as an explanation. The semi-molten asthenosphere rises with heat, causing the plates to separate, and sinks as the temperature drops, causing the plates to collide. Sometimes the edge of a plate slides under another one (subduction); pieces break off and are melted by the high temperatures. The molten material feeds volcanoes. This shrinking at the edges of the plates balances the growth at the ocean ridges.

PLOT Your Position

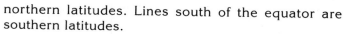

The following three activities-*Plot Your Position, Physically Featured,* and *Economically Speaking*-are a series based on the same fictitious country. Each one builds on the previous work. However, materials are included so that any one activity may be done independently of the others.

Topic
Longitude and latitude

Key Question
A new country has just been discovered. Where in the world is it?

Focus
Students plot the boundaries of a fictitious country using latitude and longitude coordinates.

Math
NCTM Standards
- *Use computation, estimation, and proportions to solve problems*
- *Use mathematics in other curriculum areas*

Estimation
Coordinates

Project 2061 Benchmarks
- *It takes two numbers to locate a point on a map or any other flat surface. The numbers may be two perpendicular distances from a point, or an angle and a distance from a point.*
- *Find and describe locations on maps with rectangular and polar coordinates.*

Social Science
Geography
  world

Processes
Predicting
Observing
Interpreting data
Making and reading maps

Materials
Rulers
World map
Optional: transparency of grid

Background Information
The Northern and Southern Hemispheres are divided by the equator. Lines north of the equator are northern latitudes. Lines south of the equator are southern latitudes.

The Eastern and Western Hemispheres are divided by the prime meridian. The 180 degree longitudinal line, which defines much of the international date line, continues this division around the world. Lines east of the prime meridian are eastern longitudes. Lines west of the prime meridian are western longitudes.

For convenience, a flat grid has been provided with equal space between each latitude and each longitude line. In actuality, longitude lines are not equidistant. See *Latitude and Longitude.*

In coordinate plotting on a graph, points along the *x*-axis are plotted first, followed by those on the *y*-axis. On a map, the latitude (*y*-axis) is plotted first and the longitude (*x*-axis) second.

Management
1. This activity may take three time periods: one to review map concepts, another for using the practice grid, and a third to plot the fictitious country.
2. Two levels of difficulty have been provided, *A* being the easier one.
3. Have students record their predictions before giving out the *Mapping Grid*. The grid gives visual clues to the country's location.
4. Some experience with *x* and *y* plotting might be helpful.
5. Check the finished map using the map in *Physically Featured.*

Procedure
1. Review map concepts (latitude, longitude, equator, prime meridian, hemispheres, direction, etc.).
2. Have students practice plotting points on either *Practice A* or *Practice B* if needed.
3. Hand out the *Mapping Sheet* first and have students record their predictions.
4. Distribute the *Mapping Grid* and allow students to plot latitudinal points independently. It may be helpful to plot the first few points on an overhead transparency to get them started.
5. Students should number each point as they plot it and connect all points, in order, with a ruler.
6. Upon completion, use a world map to see exactly where this fictitious country would lie if it existed.
7. For further map reading practice, have students cover the latitude/longitude table. Call out the various numbers (1-13) they used to label their points and have students give the latitude/longtitude readings.
8. Lead a class discussion.

Discussion

1. Does everyone have a country that is shaped exactly the same?
2. In which hemispheres does this fictitious country lie? [Southern, Western]
3. Which ocean surrounds this country? [Atlantic]
4. What is the nearest existing continent? [South America]
5. What clues in the latitude/longitude table help you establish this country's location in relation to the rest of the world? [directions, the distance of the numbers from 0 degrees latitude or longitude]
6. What is another word for 0° latitude? [equator] …for 0° longitude? [prime meridian]
7. Is it possible to live in more than one hemisphere at a time? Explain [Yes. We all live in at least two: Northern or Southern and Eastern or Western.]

Extensions

1. On a large world map, plot the points so students can visualize the location of the fictitious country in relation to the rest of the world.
2. Have students research information about the Tropic of Cancer and the Tropic of Capricorn.
3. Discuss who might have discovered this country, what kind of people might live there, and what language might be spoken.

4. Make up a name for the country.
5. Find the latitude and longitude for the city or town where you are now. What other cities or town lie along the same lines?
6. Do the follow-up activities, *Physically Featured* and *Economically Speaking*.

Curriculum Correlation

Language Arts

Write a news article, *New Country Discovered by* _____!

Math/Technology

1. Use a protractor to find the interior and exterior angles at the coordinate points.
2. Having measured the angles, use Logo to create the country on the computer.

Science

Discuss climatic differences in the Southern Hemisphere. Why are the seasons opposite to the seasons in the Northern Hemisphere?

Art

Practice A or *B* creates symmetrical patterns. Cut out or draw symmetrical pictures.

PLOT Your Position

PRACTICE A

CARTOGRAPHER _____

Plot each point and connect it to the previous point with a ruler.

Number each point as you plot it.

Note that point 1 and point 13 are the same.

LATITUDE (vertical axis): 0° 1° 2° 3° 4° 5° 6° 7° 8° 9° 10° 11° 12° 13° 14° 15° 16° 17° 18° 19° 20° 21° 22° 23° 24° 25°

LONGITUDE (horizontal axis): 1° 2° 3° 4° 5° 6° 7° 8° 9° 10° 11° 12° 13° 14° 15° 16° 17° 18° 19° 20° 21° 22° 23° 24° 25°

	LATITUDE	LONGITUDE
1.	0°	12°
2.	10°	5°
3.	10°	10°
4.	15°	5°
5.	15°	10°
6.	20°	8°
7.	20°	17°
8.	15°	15°
9.	15°	20°
10.	10°	15°
11.	10°	20°
12.	0°	13°
13.	0°	12°

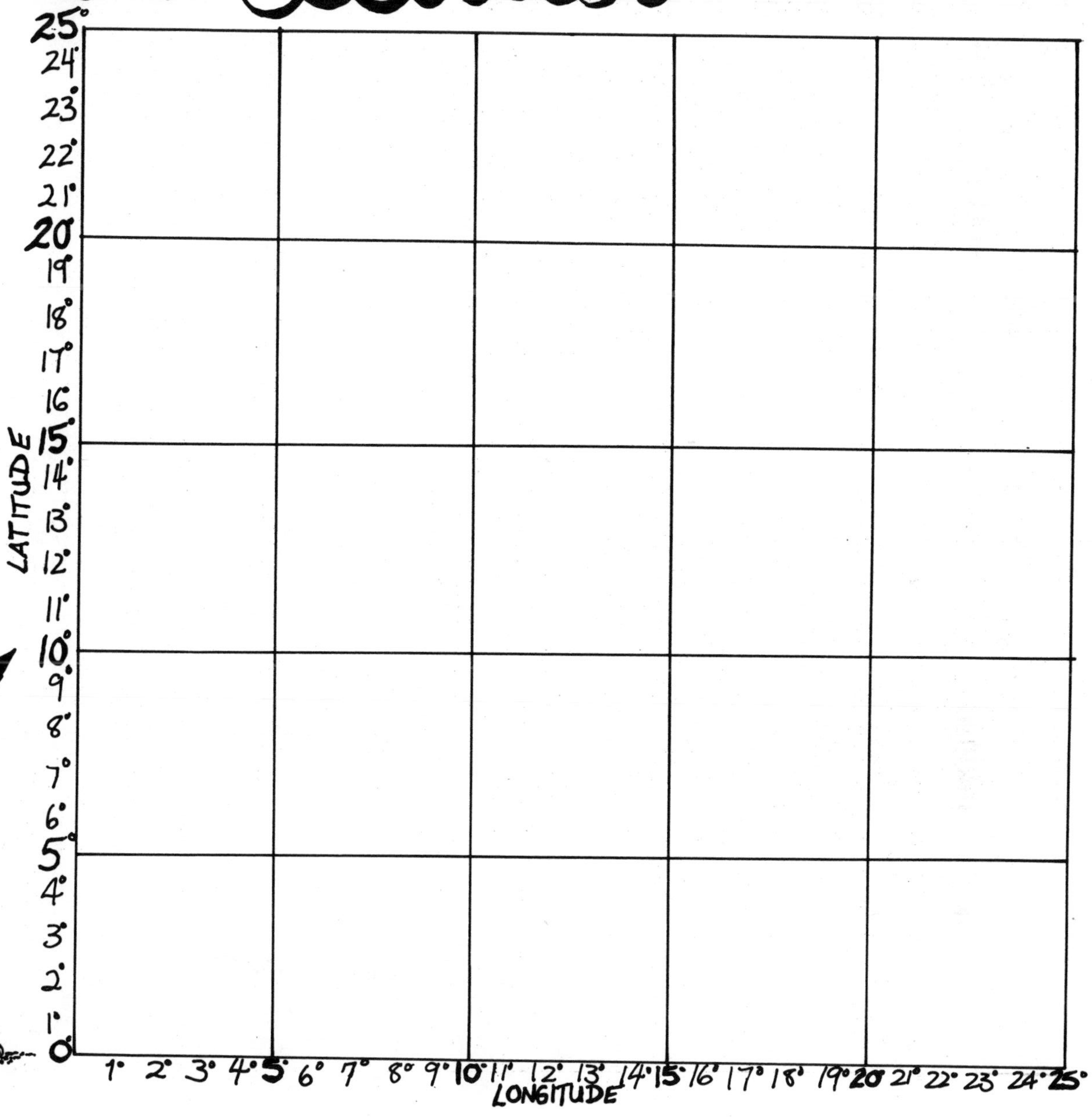

29

PLOT your Position

PRACTICE B

Plot each point and
connect it to the previous
point with a ruler.
Number each point as
you plot it.
Note that point 1 and
point 13 are the same.

	LATITUDE	LONGITUDE
1.	0°	10°
2.	1°	3°
3.	6°	8°
4.	14°	1°
5.	17°	11°
6.	22°	7°
7.	22°	18°
8	17°	14°
9.	14°	24°
10.	6°	17°
11.	1°	22°
12.	0°	15°
13	0°	10°

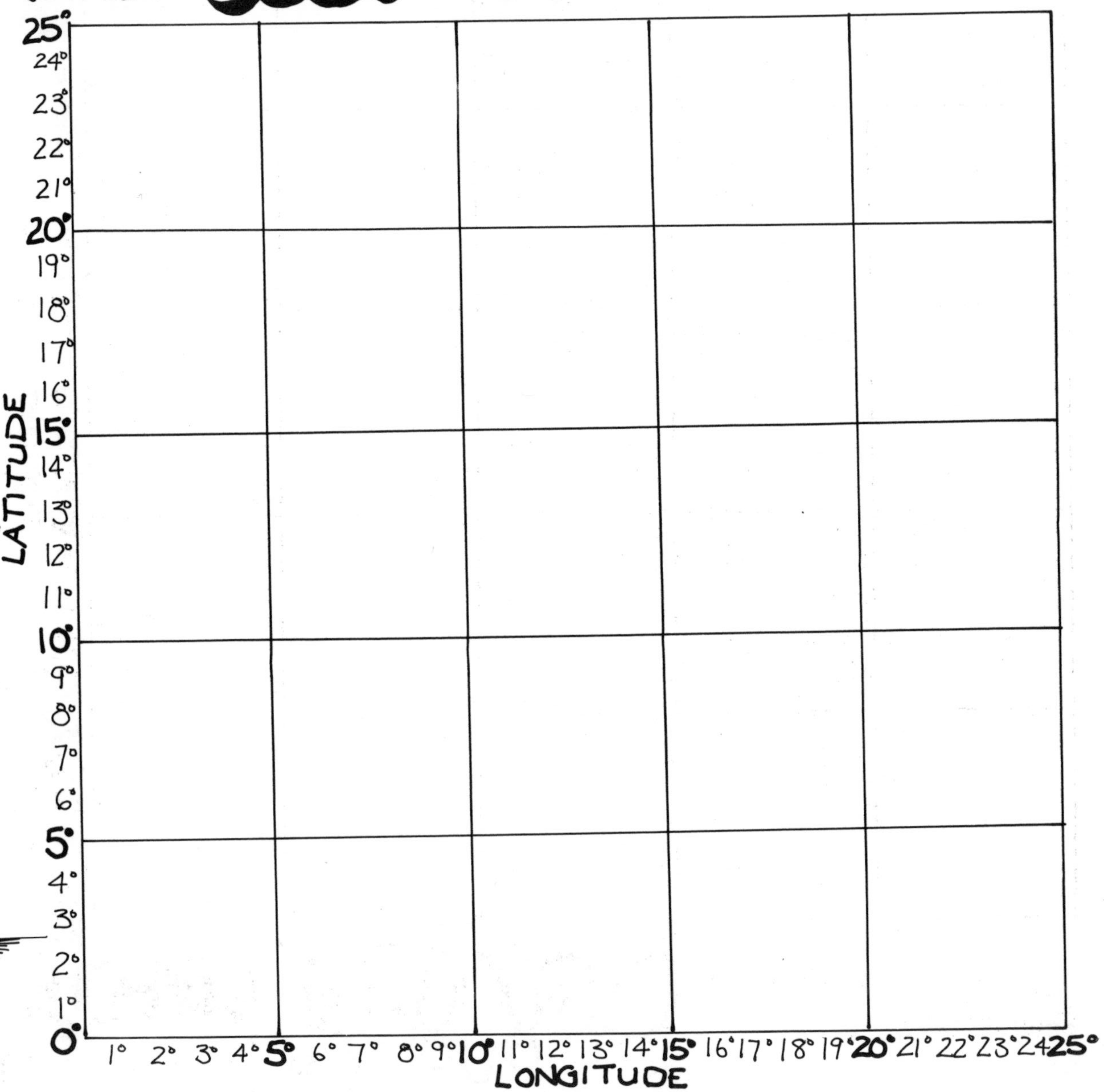

LATITUDE

25° 24° 23° 22° 21° **20°** 19° 18° 17° 16° **15°** 14° 13° 12° 11° **10°** 9° 8° 7° 6° **5°** 4° 3° 2° 1° **0°**

1° 2° 3° 4° **5°** 6° 7° 8° 9° **10°** 11° 12° 13° 14° **15°** 16° 17° 18° 19° **20°** 21° 22° 23° 24° **25°**

LONGITUDE

30

PLOT Your Position

Cartographer

Mapping Sheet A

A. Look at the points of latitude and longitude listed below. The points, when plotted and connected, will create a fictitious country located somewhere in the world.

B. Write your predictions about this fictitious country:

1. Circle the hemisphere you think that this country is in.

WEST ← NORTH EAST → SOUTH

2. Which ocean do you think it would be in? _____

3. What would the nearest continent be? _____

POINTS

	LATITUDE	LONGITUDE
1.	10° N	95° W
2.	0°	90° W
3.	5° S	75° W
4.	10° S	80° W
5.	15° S	75° W
6.	20° S	80° W
7.	25° S	85° W
8.	30° S	90° W
9.	30° S	100° W
10.	20° S	100° W
11.	20° S	110° W
12.	10° S	120° W
13.	5° S	115° W
14.	5° N	115° W
15.	0°	105° W
16.	10° N	9 5 W

C. Plot your country on the mapping grid. Connect each point to the previous point. Fill in these "facts" about your country. Use a world map.

Country's Name: _____
Hemisphere(s): _____
Ocean(s): _____
Nearest Continent: _____

Color in your country. Add towns, cities, mountains, rivers, lakes, valleys, and roads. Make a legend.

PLOT Your Position
Cartographer

Mapping Sheet B

A. Look at the points of latitude and longitude listed below. The points, when plotted and connected, will create a fictitious country located somewhere in the world.

B. Write your predictions about this fictitious country:

1. Circle the hemisphere you think that this country is in.

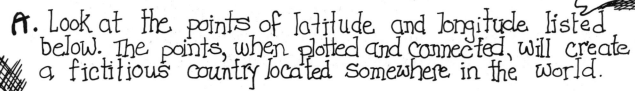

← WEST   NORTH   EAST →
SOUTH

2. Which ocean do you think it would be in? _____

3. What would the nearest continent be? _____

POINTS

	LATITUDE	LONGITUDE
1.	5° N	95° W
2.	4° N	84° W
3.	0°	80° W
4.	4° S	78° W
5.	10° S	82° W
6.	20° S	80° W
7.	22° S	90° W
8.	30° S	98° W
9.	42° S	104° W
10.	38° S	108° W
11.	30° S	106° W
12.	20° S	120° W
13.	14° S	114° W
14.	2° S	114° W
15.	2° N	104° W
16.	5° N	95° W

C. Plot your country on the mapping grid. Connect each point to the previous point. Fill in these "facts" about your country. Use a world map.

Country's Name: _____
Hemisphere(s): _____
Ocean(s): _____
Nearest Continent: _____

Color in your country. Add towns, cities, mountains, rivers, lakes, valleys, and roads. Make a legend.

MAPPING GRID A & B

10°N

0°

10°S

20°S

30°S

40°S

50°S

120°W   110°W   100°W   90°W   80°W   70°W

LATITUDE

Latitude is a measurement on a map or globe of locations north and south of the equator.

Equidistant circles are drawn parallel to the equator and to each other.

Lines of latitude are also called parallels.

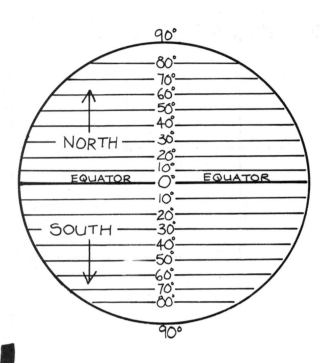

LONGITUDE

Longitude is a measurement on a map or a globe of locations east or west of the prime meridian.

The prime meridian of Greenwich was chosen as the designated imaginary north-south line that passes through both poles and Greenwich, England.

Longitude is measured 180° East and 180° West of the prime meridian.

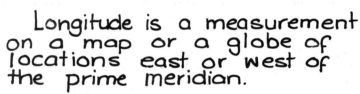

Lines of longitude are not equidistant and are also called meridians.

The combination of parallels and meridians form a grid for plotting positions anywhere in the world.

Physically Featured

Topic
Physical maps

Key Question
How does this country look from an airplane?

Focus
This activity consists of drawing the physical features of a fictitious country on a map, using coordinate directions.

Math
NCTM Standards
- *Use computation, estimation, and proportions to solve problems*
- *Use mathematics in other curriculum areas*

Estimation
Coordinates

Project 2061 Benchmarks
- *It takes two numbers to locate a point on a map or any other flat surface. The numbers may be two perpendicular distances from a point, or an angle and a distance from a point.*
- *Find and describe locations on maps with rectangular and polar coordinates.*

Social Science
Geography
world

Processes
Observing
Comparing
Interpreting data
Generalizing
Making and reading maps

Materials
Colored pencils

Background Information

This investigation may be done following *Plot Your Position* or independently. The fictitious island to be mapped is located in the southern Atlantic Ocean.

The goal is not to create identical or perfect maps. Each child's efforts are likely to be slightly different. Students will create their own physical symbols such as:

Forest	Cities
River	Mountains
Dam	Railroad
Grass	Foothills
Oil	Beach

Management
1. Use the completed *Map Grid* from *Plot Your Position* or *Map Grid A* (easier) or *B* (harder) and the corresponding *Clue Sheet* from this activity.
2. Types of maps–political, physical, topographical, weather–might be reviewed.
3. If the dam coordinates do not coincide with the river, have students place the dam across the river at a point closest to the given coordinates.
4. The forest area is more easily defined if small pencil marks are first made at each boundary point given in the directions.
5. Allow about 60 minutes for this activity.
6. Students may work independently or in small groups.
7. The maps in *Economically Speaking* can be used as an answer key.

Procedure
1. Distribute *Map Grid A* or *B* and the corresponding *Clue Sheet*. Ask the *Key Question*.
2. Have students create symbols in the *Clue Sheet* margin for later transfer to the map key.
3. Students should use a lead pencil to draw physical features on the map according to the clues given.
4. After students are satisfied with their results, they may color the map and key using colored pencils. Encourage them to make up names for the country, cities, river, etc.
5. Discuss the results with the class.

Discussion
1. Do all the maps look alike? Why or why not? [differences in estimating and symbols chosen] Compare symbols.
2. What does individual interpretation mean? How does it apply to our maps?

3. What is the difference between *approximate* and *exact*?
4. Which features could be placed exactly? [cities]
5. Which features had to be placed approximately? [rivers, mountains, etc.]
6. Is standardization of symbols important? ...Necessary? What examples of symbol standardization can you give? [road maps; road signs; symbols used in mathematics; alphabet; etc.]
7. How is a physical map useful? [travel planning – clothes needed for the terrain and climate, deciding the best form of transportation, freeway and highway route planning, etc.]

Extensions
1. Invite a surveyor to class to discuss his/her job responsibilities.
2. Reach a consensus on symbols and draw a large scale map mural.

3. Research and discuss ways a real cartographer might draw an accurate map of a country.

Curriculum Correlation
Language Arts/Art
   Use *Traveling My Way?* and sample travel brochures to help students design a brochure for this fictitious country.

Art
   Make a flour/salt relief map or papier maché model of the country.

Science
   Discuss the probable climate of this country. Give reasons.

Math
   Calculate a scale of kilometers or miles. Figure the distance between certain points in the country.

Physically Featured

Next to each clue draw the symbol you will use in your KEY.

1. There are cities located at the following points:

Latitude	Longitude
0°	90°W
10°S	90°W
20°S	100°W
10°S	120°W
30°S	90°W
15°S	110°W

2. There is a low mountain range (up to 1,200m above sea level) located along the west coast from 5°N Lat. 115°W Long. to 20°S Lat. 110W Long.

3. A river originates in the mountains at point 10°S Lat. 115°W Long. It flows eastward across the central part of the country. It passes north of the city at point 10°S Lat. 90°W Long. and continues east, where it flows into the ocean at point 5°S Lat. 75°W Long.

4. A dam has been built across the river as it flows out of the mountains at approximately 10°S Lat. 110°W Long.

5. There is a seaport located at the mouth of the river.

7. Flat grasslands cover most of the land north of the river extending to the country's northern boundary.

8. A beach resort area is located south of the forested area and along the southern boundary to point 30°S Lat. 100°W Long.

6. A large forested area is located south of the river and east of 95°W Long.

9. The area bordered by the mountains on the west, the river to the north, and the forest on the east is rolling hills, with scrub bushes and small trees.

10. A railroad runs through the forest from the beach city to the city at the mouth of the river.

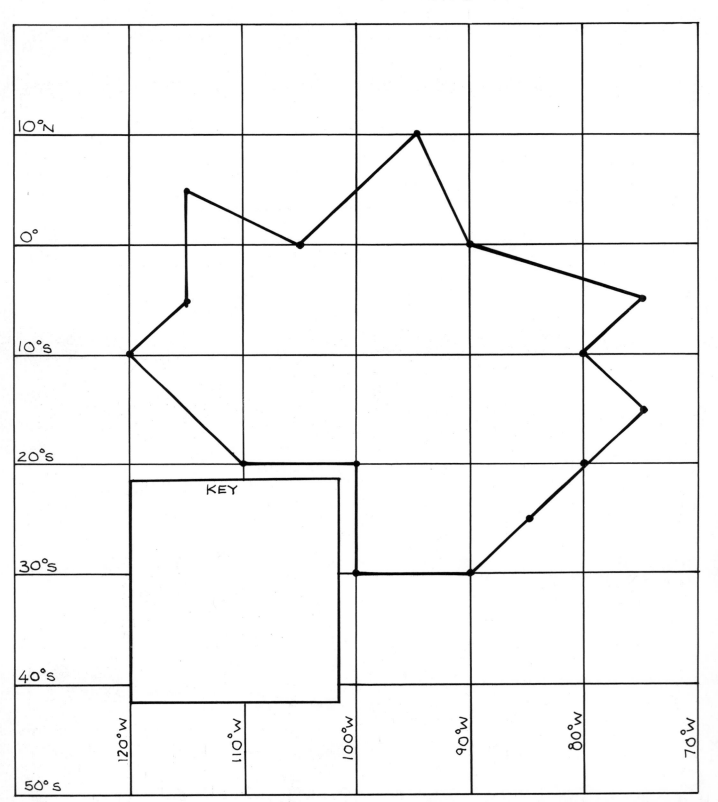

10°N
0°
10°S
20°S
30°S
40°S
50°S

120°W 110°W 100°W 90°W 80°W 70°W

KEY

Physically Featured
CLUE SHEET B

Next to each clue draw the symbol you will use in your KEY.

1. There are cities located at the following points:

Latitude	Longitude
5°N	95°W
10°S	82°W
10°S	100°W
2°S	114°W
20°S	110°W
22°S	90°W
30°S	106°W

2. There is a mountain range beginning at point 14°S Lat. 114°W Long. extending South along the west coast to point 40°S Lat. 105°W Long.
--- Height up to 3,000m ---

3. A river originates in the mountains at 18°S Lat. 114°W Long. It flows in a NE direction, passes along the SE edge of a city, continues to 15°S Lat. 90°W Long., then turns in a SE direction until it empties into the ocean at 10°S Lat. 82°W Long.

4. A dam has been built across the river at 12°S Lat. 106°W Long.

5. An extensive forested area is located south of the river approximately between the following points:

Latitude	Longitude
7°S	90°W
12°S	97°W
15°S	84°W
20°S	91°W
31°S	100°W
20°S	100°W

6. The land north of the river, extending to the northern boundary, is flat grassland with rich soil.

7. Off-shore drilling exists at 38°S Lat. 110°W Long.

8. The triangular area between the river, forest, and mountains is hilly land with scrub bushes and low trees.

9. A beautiful stretch of sandy beach is located between 22°S Lat. 90°W Long. and 20°S Lat. 80°W Long.

10. A railroad connects the city at 30°S Lat. 106°W Long. with the beach resort. It then continues on to the city at the mouth of the river.

11. Two other rail lines leave the city at the mouth of the river. One goes to the city furthest north, the second goes to the city furthest west.

Physically Featured

MAPPING GRID B

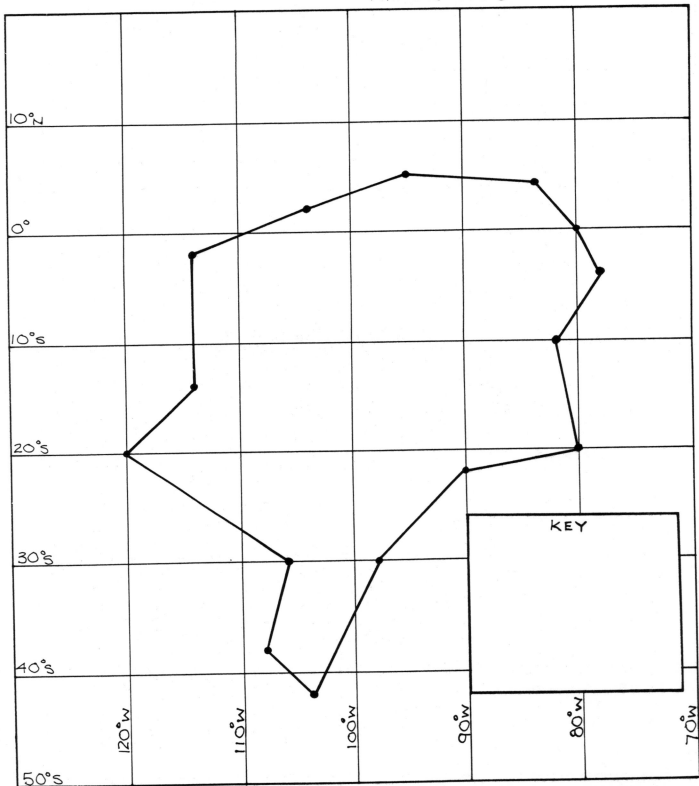

10°N

0°

10°S

20°S

30°S

40°S

50°S

120°W 110°W 100°W 90°W 80°W 70°W

KEY

TRAVELING MY WAY ?

PHYSICALLY FEATURED

Design a travel brochure to interest people in visiting your country.

Include:

- pictures with captions

- special features

- recreation such as swimming, hiking, or fishing

- cultural events such as plays or concerts

- historical sites (Here's your chance to make history.)

- transportation (how to get there)

You will want to name the important features.

Economically $peaking

Topic
Land use

Key Question
What physical features give clues to a country's economy?

Focus
Students infer and draw conclusions about the economy of a country based on its physical features.

Math
NCTM Standards
- *Compute with whole numbers, fractions, decimals, integers, and rational numbers*
- *Construct, read, and interpret tables, charts and graphs*
- *Extend their understanding of the concepts of perimeter, area, volume, angle measure, capacity, and weight and mass*
- *Make and use estimates of measurement*

Estimation
　rounding
Measurement
　area
　length
　angle
Whole number operations
Ratios
Decimals
Percent
Graphs
　pictograph
　circle

Project 2061 Benchmarks
- *Seek better reasons for believing something than "Everybody knows that ..." or "I just know" and discount such reasons when given by others.*
- *Areas of irregular shapes can be found by dividing them into squares and triangles.*
- *Trade between nations occurs when natural resources are unevenly distributed and the costs of production are very different in different countries. A nation has a trade opportunity whenever it can create more of a product or service at a lower cost than another.*

Social Science
Economics
Geography

Processes
Observing
Classifying
Comparing
Interpreting data
Inferring
Generalizing
Working cooperatively
Communicating ideas
Reading maps

Materials
Calculators
Protractors
Rulers
Colored pencils or crayons

Background Information
　If this activity is done independently of *Physically Featured*, students will need to know that they are dealing with a fictitious country located in the southern Atlantic Ocean.

　When discussing inferences, encourage students to give sound reasons for their choices. Some possible inferences:

Cities:	small businesses, tourism, manufacturing
Mountains:	mining, paper production, tourism
River/Dam:	electric power, farm crops, ranching, paper production, fishing
Forests:	paper production, some livestock
Grasslands:	farming, livestock
Hilly Land:	ranching
Beach:	tourism
Railroad:	farm crops, ranching, paper production, manufacturing, mining, textiles
Ocean:	fishing, tourism, drilling for oil

　Estimation is needed when finding the area of each physical feature. If more than half the square contains the feature, count it as a whole square. *Map A* has approximately 250 squares and *Map B*, 275 squares. Students should count all the way to the edge of the physical feature and/or the country. Expect the total to be less accurate than counting the number of squares in the entire country.

　The GNP or Gross National Product as defined by the *Encyclopedia Britannica* "...is the total market value of the final goods and services produced by a nation's economy during a specific period of time (usually a year), computed before allowance is made for the depreciation or consumption of capital used in the process of production." NNP or Net National

Product would be computed after such an allowance was made.

Management
1. This activity has three parts: 1) making inferences 2) finding areas and 3) constructing the circle graph.
2. Use the completed *Map Grid* from *Physically Featured* or *Map Grid A* (easier) or *B* (harder) from this activity.
3. Groups of four promote discussion of ideas, particularly when making inferences. The groups can continue to work together throughout the activity, but each member should be required to complete a circle graph and possibly the pictograph.
4. Symbols on the pictograph must be evenly spaced.
5. The *Circle Graph* lists arbitrary percentages that are realistic for the physical makeup of the country. Students should round the number of degrees to the nearest whole.

Procedure
1. Give out *Map Grid A* or *B* and ask the *Key Question*. Have students make a list, on scratch paper, of anything they feel this country might produce based on its physical features.
2. Distribute the *Inference* sheet to each small group and have them complete it. Discuss choices as a class.
3. Hand out the *Area* sheet and *Graph Grid*. Students should hold the paper up to a window or light, if necessary, and count the squares to find the area covered by each physical feature. Each square equals one kilometer. (Hint: 25 squares equal one square on the latitude/longitude grid.)
4. Have students complete the area table and illustrate the data on a pictograph.
5. Discuss ways to find the lengths requested at the bottom of the *Area* sheet [use the edge of the graph paper].
6. Instruct students to compute the number of degrees representing each economic factor for *Map Grid A* or *Map Grid B* and illustrate on a circle graph.
7. Hold a concluding discussion.

Discussion
1. Do the physical features of a country affect its economy? How?
2. Which physical features provide for the various economic factors presented on the *Inference* sheet? [See *Background Information*.]
3. What type of products do you think this country might export?
4. What products might this country need to import?
5. Would this country attract a lot of tourists? Why or why not? Is it near major shipping or air lanes?

Extensions
1. Use the list of major economic factors to determine specifics regarding this country's economy. For example, manufacturing might include cheese production from dairy farms, textiles from cotton, meat processing plants from ranching, paper mills from lumber, etc.
2. Contact a travel agent to establish existing cruise lines and airlines that currently operate in the area of the fictitious country. Draw a map showing where flights and cruises might originate.
3. Compare the economy of this fictitious country to another in the same part of the world.
4. Research the division of the U.S. economy and illustrated with a circle graph.

Curriculum Correlation
Language Arts
   Write an article describing the types of jobs available for someone who might want to move to this country.

Science
   Research the types of marine life to be found in this area of the world. Add drawings of these to the map.

Art
   Make a scale model of this country using material from nature.

Music
   Make up a national anthem.

Economically $peaking

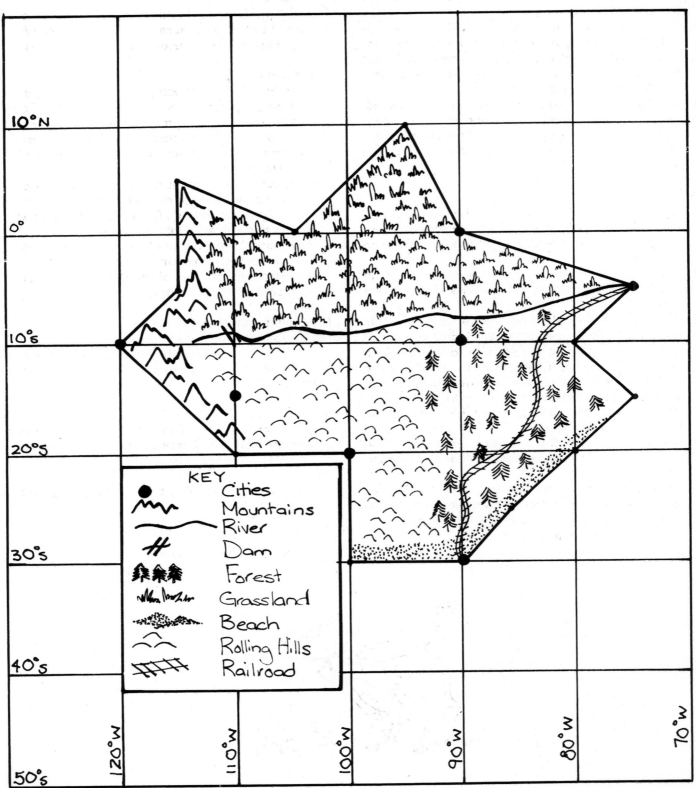

10°N

0°

10°S

20°S

KEY
- ● Cities
- Mountains
- River
- Dam
- Forest
- Grassland
- Beach
- Rolling Hills
- Railroad

30°S

40°S

50°S

120°W   110°W   100°W   90°W   80°W   70°W

Economically $peaking

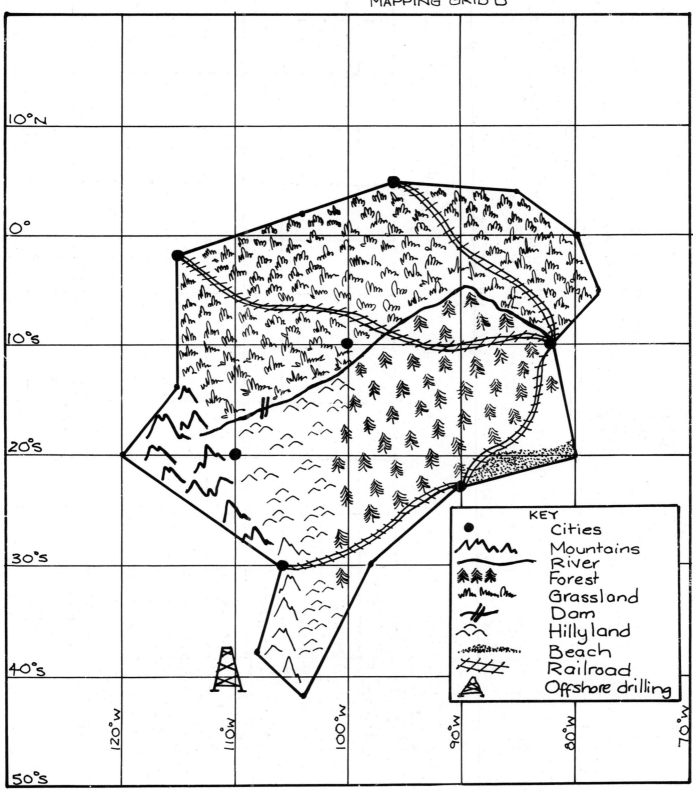

KEY

●	Cities
Mountains	Mountains
River	River
Forest	Forest
Grassland	Grassland
Dam	Dam
Hillyland	Hillyland
Beach	Beach
Railroad	Railroad
Offshore drilling	Offshore drilling

10°N
0°
10°S
20°S
30°S
40°S
50°S

120°W 110°W 100°W 90°W 80°W 70°W

45

Economically $peaking
A & B

Economic Prognosticators

Place a "Y" for YES in each box where you think the physical feature would support the economic factor. Be ready to offer reasons for your choices.

ECONOMIC FACTORS

PHYSICAL FEATURES	ELECTRIC POWER	DAIRY FARMING	FARM CROPS	RANCHING	PAPER PRODUCTION	FISHING	SMALL BUSINESSES	TOURISM	MANUFACTURING	MINING	DRILLING FOR OIL	TEXTILES
CITIES												
MOUNTAINS												
RIVER												
FOREST												
GRASSLANDS												
HILLY LAND												
BEACH												
RAILROAD												
OCEAN												
DAM												

Economically $peaking

GRAPH GRID

One square = One square kilometer

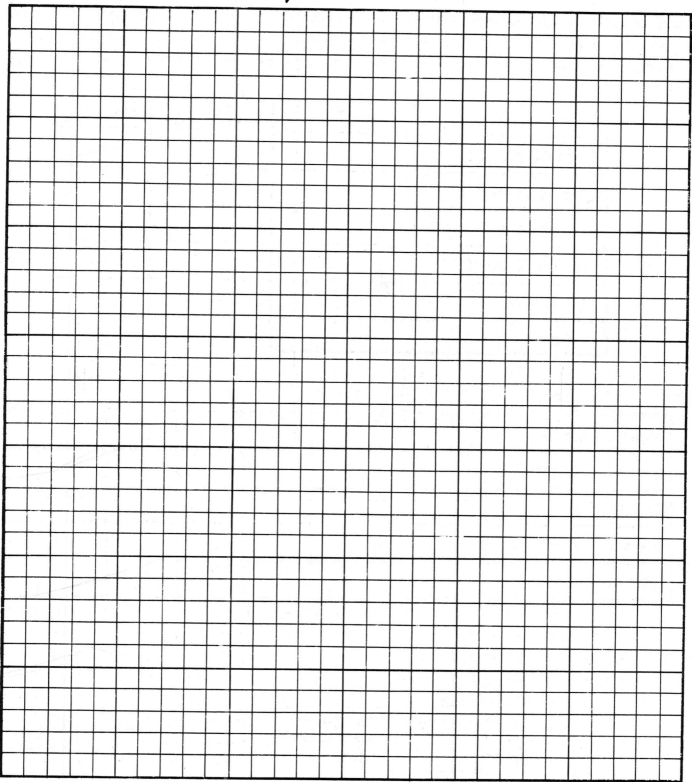

AREA

1. Place the graph paper behind your map. Count the approximate number of square kilometers of each feature. Total these numbers to find the approximate area (km²) of the entire country. Complete the chart below.

	KM²	$\frac{KM^2}{TOTAL\ KM^2}$	PERCENT
MOUNTAINS			
GRASSLANDS			
FORESTS			
HILLY LAND			
BEACH			
TOTAL			

2. Use the information above to create a pictograph!

MOUNTAINS														
GRASSLANDS														
FORESTS														
HILLY LAND														
BEACH														

10 20 30 40 50 60 70 80 90 100 110 120 130 140 150
KM²

3. How many kilometers?

River_____

Railroad _____

Country at widest point_____

Country at longest point_____

Shore to drilling site _____
(B only)

Economically $peaking

CIRCLE GRAPH

Complete the table.
Round degrees.

$$\frac{(\% \div 100)}{\text{Percent in decimal form}} \times \frac{360}{\text{Degrees in Circle}} = \frac{}{\text{\# of degrees}}$$

MAP A ONLY

ECONOMIC FACTOR	% OF GNP	# OF DEGREES
LIVESTOCK	10%	
AGRICULTURE	20%	
MINING	10%	
TIMBER-RELATED INDUSTRY	25%	
FISHING-RELATED INDUSTRY	15%	
MANUFACTURING	15%	
TOURISM	1%	
OTHER	4%	

MAP B ONLY

ECONOMIC FACTOR	% OF GNP	# OF DEGREES
LIVESTOCK	6%	
AGRICULTURE	23%	
MINING	5%	
TIMBER-RELATED INDUSTRY	15%	
FISHING-RELATED INDUSTRY	25%	
MANUFACTURING	7%	
PETROLEUM	14%	
TOURISM	2%	
OTHER	3%	

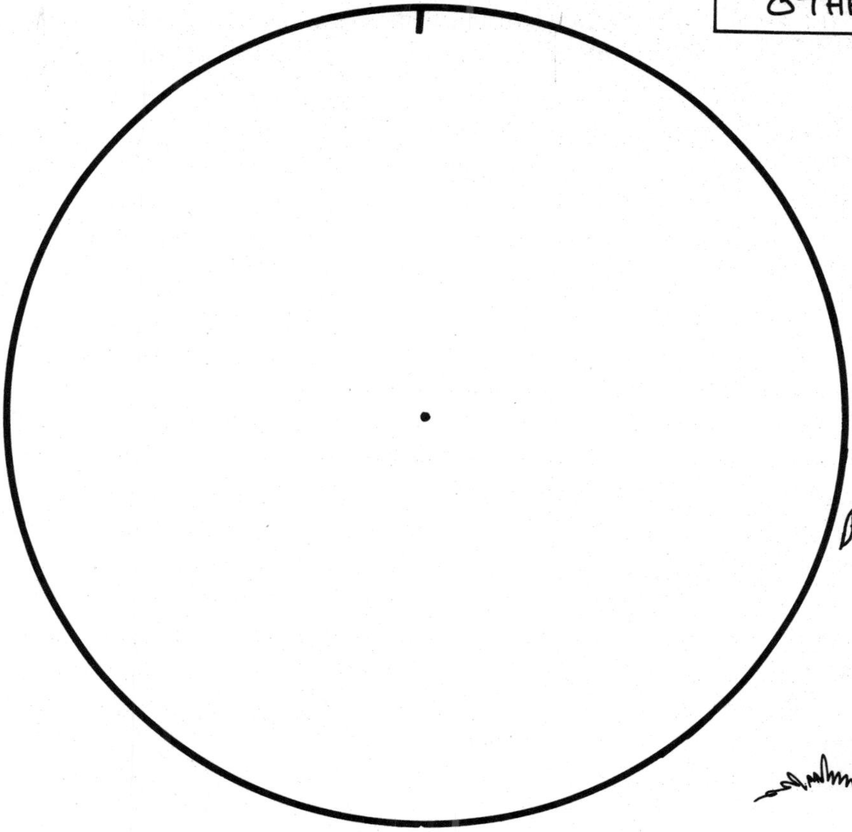

Use the above information to draw a circle graph depicting the GNP for MAP A or MAP B. Color and label each part.

49

I'VE GOT THE WORLD ON A STRING

Topic
Distances on a globe

Key Question
How can we find distances on a globe?

Focus
Students use a string and calculations to determine the distances between two points on a globe.

Math
NCTM Standards
- *Estimate, make, and use measurements to describe and compare phenomena*
- *Use computation, estimation, and proportions to solve problems*
- *Understand and apply ratios, proportions, and percents in a wide variety of situations*

Estimation
  rounding
Measurement
  length
Whole number operations
Ratio and proportion
Decimals

Project 2061 Benchmarks
- *Scale drawings show shapes and compare locations of things very different in size.*
- *Use numerical data in describing and comparing objects and events.*
- *Estimate distances and travel times from maps and the actual size of objects from scale drawings.*

Social Science
Geography
  world

Processes
Observing
Collecting and recording data
Comparing
Interpreting data
Inferring
Generalizing

Working cooperatively
Communicating ideas
Reading maps

Materials
For the class:
  kilometer post materials (see *Background Information*)
For each group:
  string with no elasticity, about 1 meter long
  1 meter tape
  1 globe (sizes need not be the same)

Background Information
PROPORTION
  Each map or globe is drawn to a scale. Because this scale is consistent throughout a particular map or globe, it can be matched with the actual measurements of the earth.

  How is the formula for converting string length to kilometers determined? First find the globe's circumference by measuring the equator in centimeters. Then stretch a string between two cities on any globe. Mark the string with a pencil or knots and measure the centimeter distance (to the nearest tenth) with a meter tape. Set up a ratio:

  Measured distance between
    2 points on a globe   →   16.2 cm
    Circumference of globe   →   118 cm

  Relate this ratio to a similar ratio of the actual kilometers. The earth's circumference at the equator is 40,075 km (24,900 miles). The unknown is the actual distance between the two cities. When the two ratios are used together, it is called a proportion. With three pieces of information, it can be solved for x. For example:
  Set up the proportion.
  $$\frac{16.2 \text{ cm}}{118 \text{ cm}} = \frac{x}{40,075 \text{km}}$$

  Cross multiply.
  $118x = 16.2 \times 40,075$
  $118x = 649,215$

  Isolate x by dividing
  $x = 649,215 \div 118$
  $x = 5,502$ km

THE KILOMETER POST

Materials: For an outside post, use a tetherball pole and attach cardboard, plywood, or plastic markers. For an inside post, insert a cylindrical object such as a broomstick, pipe, or several connected mailing tubes into a Christmas tree stand. Attach arrow signs.

Gathering Information: Measure from a common starting point, most likely your city. Decide the cities to be included on the kilometer post; consider those currently in the news or part of the curriculum. Find the distance between the starting point and each chosen city by measuring on the globe. Also determine the N, S, E, W, NW, SW, NE, or SE direction of this city from the starting point. Make directional signs (North/South, East/West) and mount on top of the post. Attach city signs to the kilometer post, facing in the proper directions.

Management

1. This activity can be divided into three parts: 1) measuring and finding proportions 2) searching the globe for answers to the open-ended questions and 3) constructing the kilometer post.
2. Groups of four or five are recommended, depending on how many globes are available. Job descriptions such as City Locator, String Stretcher, Mathematician, Estimator, and Recorder could be used so that all members of the team have a specific job.
3. Have students do the *Estimated km* column, one at a time. The first estimate will probably be a blind guess. After finding the actual kilometers, have them make their next estimate. Experience should improve accuracy. Also stress accurate measurements.
4. When building a class kilometer post, each group should contribute at least two arrow signs showing city and distance. The direction may be penciled in on the back so proper placement can be made.
5. Representatives from each group should build the post while individual groups are making their arrow signs.

Procedure

1. Ask the *Key Question*.
2. Distribute the first activity sheet and have each group measure around the equator of their globe in centimeters.
3. Students should then estimate and record the number of kilometers from New York to San Francisco.
4. After guiding a study of the proportion at the top of the page, have students use string to measure the distance between the two cities, complete the proportion, and find the actual kilometers.
5. Instruct students to follow the same procedure to complete the rest of the table.
6. Discuss the results.

7. Hand out the second and third activity sheets. Have groups explore and record answers to the questions.
8. Students should share their findings.
9. Have the class construct the kilometer post and decide the cities to be listed on it.
10. Each student group should be responsible for gathering data, designing, and placing two or more signs on the post.

Discussion

1. Why is using a non-rigid measuring device beneficial when determining distances on a globe? [It can be placed along a curve.]
2. Why are the distances measured by a string not accurate for determining driving miles? [Bodies of water and land forms such as mountains cause land routes to be altered.] Relate to question seven on the kilometer post sheet.
3. Why is a polar route preferable when flying to some Asian or European countries? [shorter distances, less air traffic than when flying over populated areas]
4. Why do people in Alaska have air travel benefits that people in the continental U.S. do not have? [Since they are closer to the North Pole, the polar route allows them to travel a shorter distance to places in the Northern Hemisphere.]
5. When planning a trip, why is knowing how to determine approximate distances necessary? [to approximate expenses and plan for journey time]
6. Why is this form of measuring distances accurate whatever the size of the globe used? [Every globe is drawn to scale. This consistency makes it possible to compare the actual size of the earth to any globe.]

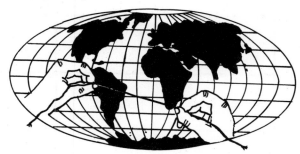

Extensions

1. Invite a pilot to discuss how air routes are determined.
2. Brainstorm factors important when planning a long distance trip. Then invite a travel agent to speak about trip planning.
3. Plan a trip around the world. Determine stopover points and calculate the total distance to be traveled.
4. Try another kind of activity about the shortest distance between two map points. See *Thumbtack Sandwich II* from the AIMS book, *Soap Films and Bubbles*.

I'VE GOT THE WORLD ON A STRING

Names
_____
_____
_____
_____

1. Measure the equator of your globe. The circumference is _____ cm.

2. Use this proportion to find the distance between any two points on your globe:

$$\frac{\text{Distance between 2 pts. on globe (cm)}}{\text{Circumference of globe (cm)}} = \frac{\text{(Actual distance between 2 pts.)} \quad X}{\textbf{40,075 km} \text{ (Actual circumference of the earth)}}$$

CITIES	ESTIMATED KM	PROPORTION	ACTUAL KM
New York/San Francisco		——— = ——— 40,075	
Seattle / Miami		——— = ———	
Anchorage/ Tokyo		——— = ———	
Cairo / Perth		——— = ———	
Bogata /Capetown		——— = ———	
		——— = ———	
		——— = ———	

I'VE GOT THE WORLD ON A STRING

1. Measure the equator of your globe. The circumference is _____ cm.

2. Use this proportion to find the distance between any two points on your globe:

$$\frac{\text{Distance between 2 pts. on globe (cm)}}{\text{Circumference of globe (cm)}} = \frac{\text{(Actual distance between 2 pts.)} \quad X}{40,075 \text{ km} \text{ (Actual circumference of the earth)}}$$

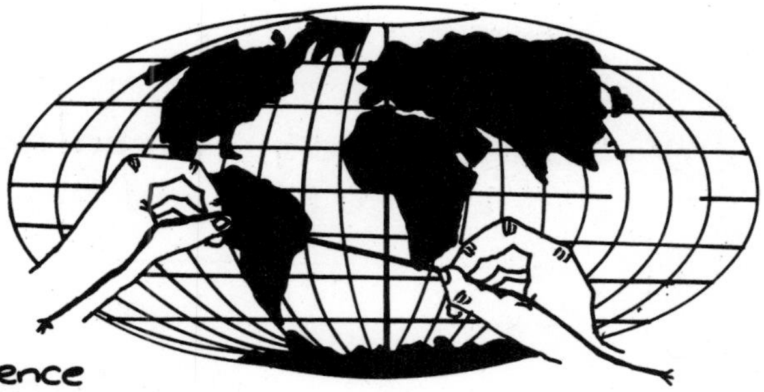

3. Find pairs of cities separated by about 2,000 km. Name each city and country. How many cm is 2,000 km on your globe? _____ cm

_____ and _____

_____ and _____

4. Find pairs of cities 10,000 km apart. What is the measure of 10,000 km on your globe? _____

_____ and _____

_____ and _____

5. Find pairs of cities _____ km apart. They would measure _____ on my globe.

_____ and _____

_____ and _____

6. Find two cities separated by the same distance as Lima, Peru and San Francisco, United States. What is the measured distance on your globe? _____. What is the actual kilometer distance? _____

_____ and _____

I'VE GOT THE WORLD ON A STRING

7. As the crow flies, the distance from Washington D.C. to San Francisco is about 3,930 kilometers (2,440 miles). The driving distance is about 4,720km (2,930miles). What factors would cause the difference?

8. Why do people in Alaska have air travel benefits that people in the continental U.S. do not have?

CONSTRUCT A KILOMETER POST

1. Common starting point: _____

CITIES	KM	DIRECTION FROM STARTING POINT

2.

Honolulu 4,400 km

Chicago 3440 km

Dallas 2,130 km

3. Place East-West/North-South arrows at the top of the post. Attach city signs facing the proper direction.

South American Jigsaw

Topic
South American countries

Key Question
How do the countries of South America fit together?

Focus
Students will place the South American countries in the proper geographical positions by using clues requiring inductive reasoning.

Math
NCTM Standard
- *Recognize and apply deductive and inductive reasoning*

Problem solving

Logic

Project 2061 Benchmark
- *Offer reasons for their findings and consider reasons suggested by others.*

Social Science
Geography
world

Processes
Observing
Comparing
Interpreting data
Working cooperatively
Communicating ideas
Making maps

Materials
Scissors
Glue

Background Information
This activity might be used as an introduction to the study of South American geography or history. The map should look like the one shown.

Inductive reasoning involves moving from the specific to the general. In its truest sense, a generalization is formed based on a few specific examples. This often happens in the scientific process. This activity uses a broader form of inductive reasoning. It starts with clues about the positions of individual countries relative to each other and results in a visual generalization of the political boundaries of South America.

Management
1. Prior experience with logic and inductive reasoning is helpful.
2. It is essential that students know the position of the three bodies of water (Caribbean Sea, Atlantic Ocean, and Pacific Ocean) which surround South America.
3. Groups of four are suggested. Cut the clue cards apart so they can be distributed to individual group members.
4. This activity will take 30 minutes or more.

Procedure
1. Ask the *Key Question* and give each student group the countries and the outline map. Have them cut out the thirteen countries.
2. Students should label the Pacific Ocean, Atlantic Ocean, Caribbean Sea, and compass rose on the outline map.
3. Distribute the clue cards to individual group members. Have students use the countries, the outline map, and the clues to correctly assemble the continent. <u>At the group's request, clues can be read aloud any number of times but may not be passed to other members</u>. No resource maps allowed!
4. Instruct students to glue the assembled countries onto the outline map after checking the clues to make sure they match the map.
5. Lead a class discussion.

Discussion
1. What clues were most helpful in getting started?
2. Describe how you solved the problem. In what order did you work?
3. What country did you find the hardest to locate? Why?
4. What, if anything, was frustrating? Explain.

Extensions
1. Using physical and political maps, draw and label the major cities, rivers, and mountains of South America. Draw the equator.
2. Do *A Patch of North America*.

Curriculum Correlation
Language Arts/Logic/Geography

Make a set of clues for arranging the provinces of Canada or placing the physical landmarks (mountains, valleys, national parks, lakes, etc.) in a state.

South American Jigsaw

CLUE CARDS

Cut these cards apart and distribute them to individual group members.

---

7. The countries bordering the Atlantic Ocean are Uruguay, Guyana, Argentina, Suriname, Brazil, and French Guiana.

8. Colombia touches Central America.

9. Venezuela and Colombia border each other and the Caribbean Sea.

---

10. Ecuador is between Colombia and Peru.

11. Bolivia is farther northwest than Paraguay.

12. Guyana is on the eastern border of Venezuela and north of Brazil.

REVIEW THE CLUES TO MAKE SURE THEY AGREE WITH YOUR COMPLETED MAP.

---

1. Brazil borders all the countries except Ecuador and Chile.

2. The countries bordering the Pacific Ocean are Chile, Peru, Colombia, and Ecuador.

3. Bolivia and Paraguay are the only countries not bordering an ocean.

---

4. Argentina and Chile are the farthest south of all the countries.

5. Argentina is bordered by Chile, Bolivia, Paraguay, Brazil, Uruguay, and the Atlantic Ocean.

6. Suriname is located between French Guiana and Guyana.

South American Jigsaw

Cut out these countries.

South American Jigsaw

Label the Pacific Ocean, Atlantic Ocean, Caribbean Sea, and the compass rose.

A patch of North America

Topic
Lower countries of North America

Key Question
Where in the world is Belize (bəlēz´)?

Focus
Students will place the North American countries in the proper geographical positions using clues requiring inductive reasoning.

Math
NCTM Standard
- *Recognize and apply deductive and inductive reasoning*

Problem solving
Logic

Project 2061 Benchmark
- *Offer reasons for their findings and consider reasons suggested by others.*

Social Science
Geography
  world

Processes
Observing
Comparing
Interpreting data
Working cooperatively
Communicating ideas
Making maps

Materials
Scissors
Glue

Background Information
This introduction to the geography of North and Central America, an important region in current events, should result in a map like the one shown above.

Inductive reasoning involves moving from the specific to the general. In its truest sense, a generalization is formed based on a few specific examples. This often happens in the scientific process. This activity uses a broader form of inductive reasoning. It starts with clues about the positions of individual countries relative to each other and results in a visual generalization of the political boundaries of North America.

Management
1. Logic and inductive reasoning experience is helpful.
2. Students must know the location of the Pacific Ocean, Atlantic Ocean, Caribbean Sea, and Gulf of Mexico.
3. Groups of four are suggested. Cut the clue cards apart so they can be distributed to individual group members.
4. This activity will take 30 minutes or more.

Procedure
1. Ask the *Key Question* and give each student group the countries and the outline map. Have them glue the map together and cut out the countries.
2. Students should label the Pacific Ocean, Atlantic Ocean, Caribbean Sea, Gulf of Mexico, and compass rose on the outline map.
3. Distribute the clue cards to individual group members. Have students use the countries, the outline map, and the clues to correctly assemble the continent. <u>At the group's request, clues can be read aloud any number of times but may not be passed to other members</u>. No resource maps allowed!
4. Instruct students to glue the assembled countries onto the outline map after checking the clues to make sure they match the map.
5. Lead a class discussion.

Discussion
1. What country was hardest for you to locate? Why?
2. Why is it important to know where these countries are located? [Fast transportation and instant communication have made the world seem much smaller and closer to us. Literate people need to know about their neighbors; important world events take place in these countries.]

Extensions
1. Using physical and political maps, draw and label the major cities, rivers, and mountains of North America.
2. Do *South American Jigsaw*.

Curriculum Correlation
Language Arts/Logic/Geography

Write a set of clues for arranging countries in another part of the world, placing the physical landmarks in a state, locating rooms within a building, or finding places of interest in a city. For example, if the class is reading *From the Mixed-Up Files of Mrs. Basil E. Frankweiler* by E.L. Konigsburg, the layout of one floor of the Metropolitan Museum of Art in New York City might be an interesting challenge.

A Patch of North America

CLUE CARDS

Cut these cards apart and distribute them to individual group members.

1. Panama touches Colombia.

2. Guatemala is on the southern border of Mexico.

3. Nicaragua borders Honduras.

4. Puerto Rico is the easternmost island shown in the Caribbean Sea.

5. Belize and El Salvador both border Guatemala.

6. Costa Rica is one country away from South America.

7. Cuba is directly south of a peninsula in the United States.

8. Almost all of the beaches in Honduras are along the Caribbean Sea.

9. Haiti and the Dominican Republic share an island. Of the two, Haiti is closer to Mexico.

10. The Pacific Ocean touches the western coast of El Salvador.

11. Jamaica is directly north of Panama.

12. Mexico is between the Pacific Ocean and the Gulf of Mexico.

REVIEW THE CLUES TO MAKE SURE THEY AGREE WITH YOUR COMPLETED MAP.

A patch of North America

Cut out these countries.

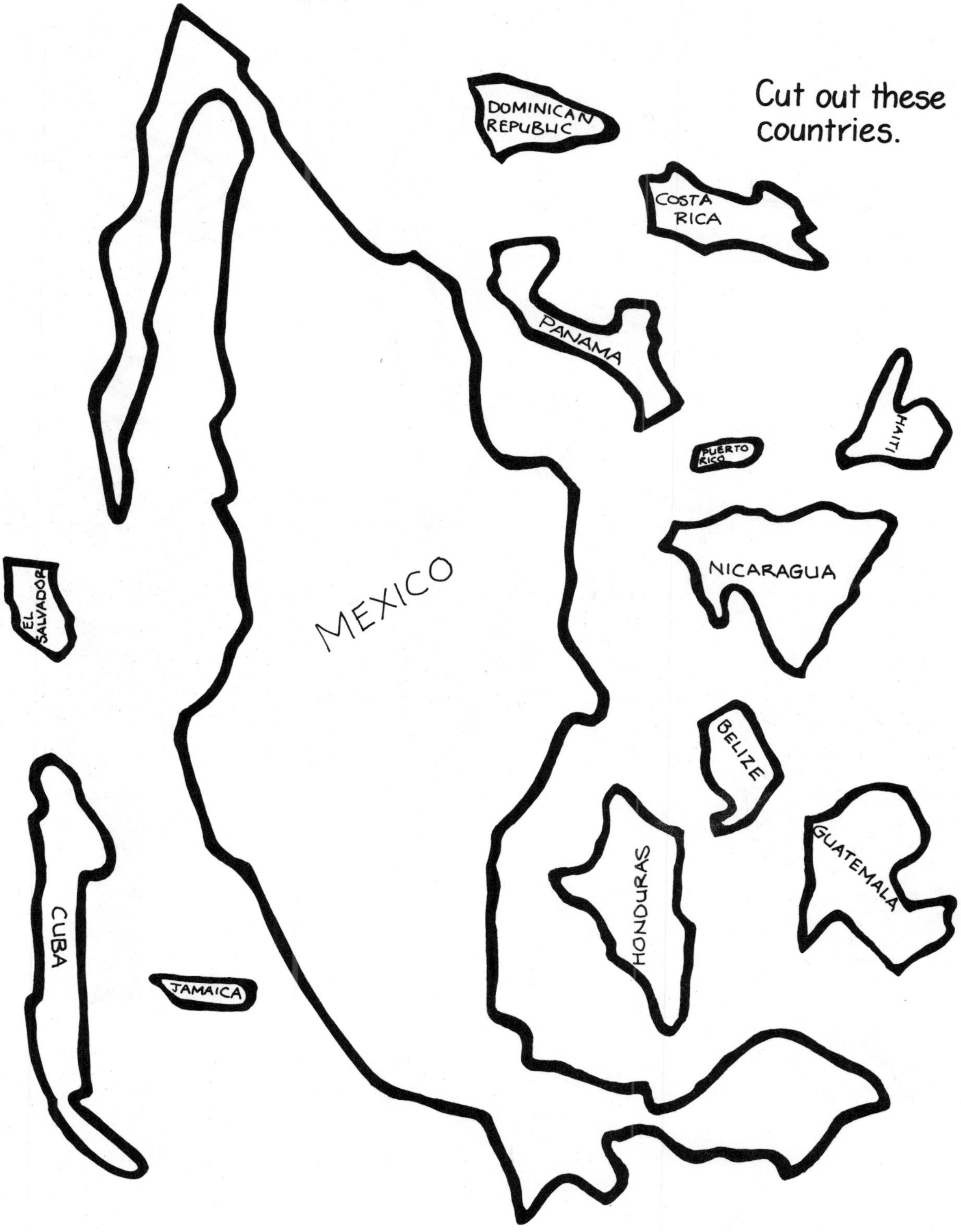

DOMINICAN REPUBLIC

COSTA RICA

PANAMA

HAITI

PUERTO RICO

NICARAGUA

MEXICO

EL SALVADOR

BELIZE

GUATEMALA

HONDURAS

CUBA

JAMAICA

Cut along dotted line and glue, matching along solid line.

A Patch of North America
SOUTH AMERICA

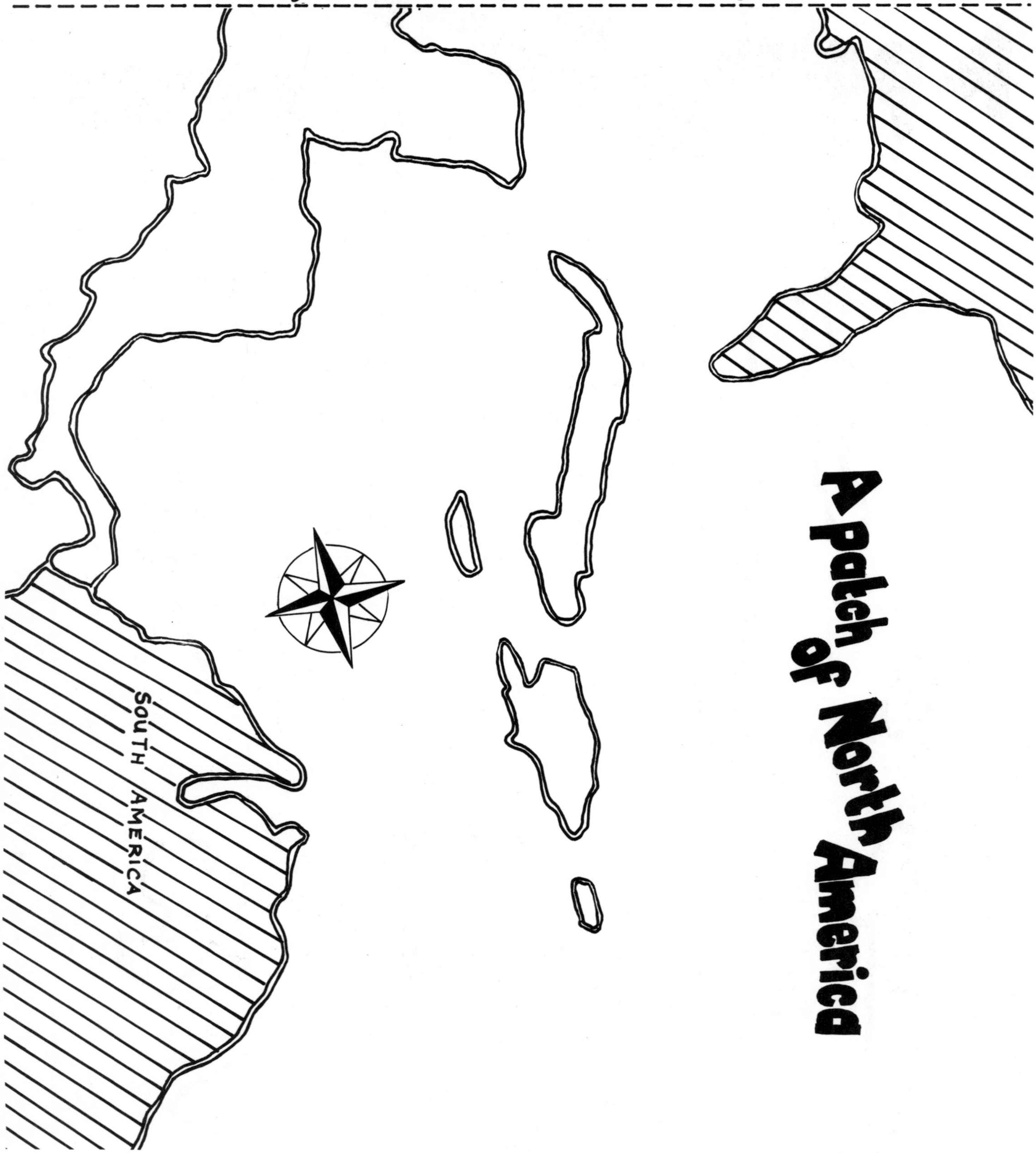

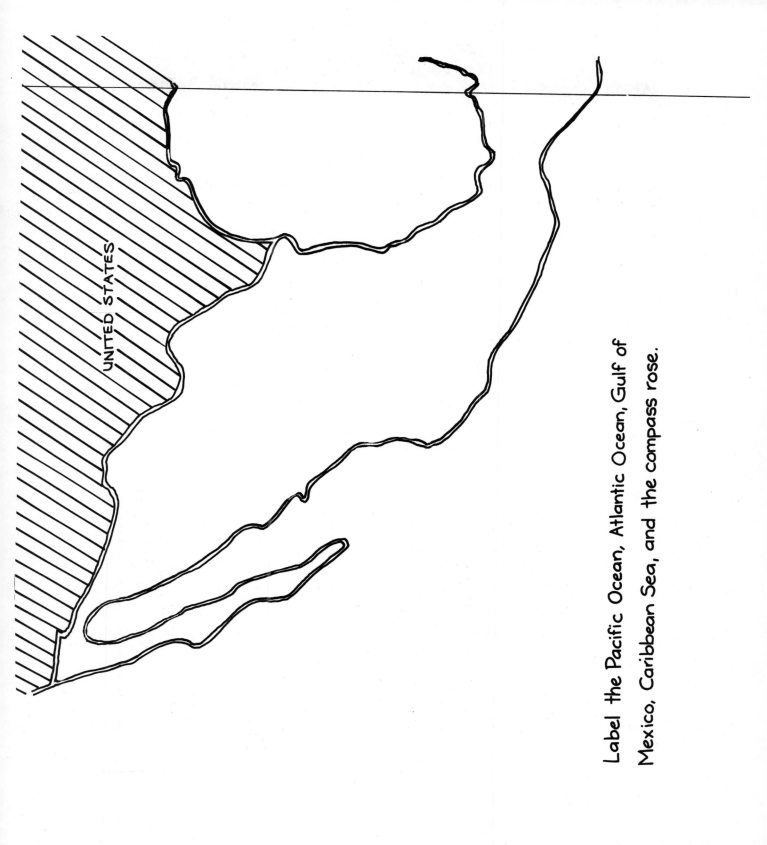

UNITED STATES

Label the Pacific Ocean, Atlantic Ocean, Gulf of Mexico, Caribbean Sea, and the compass rose.

63

Getting There

Topic
Compass directions

Key Question
How can you avoid getting lost?

Focus
Students will use compass directions to create a scale map of the playground.

Math
NCTM Standards
- *Understand and apply ratios, proportions, and percents in a wide variety of situations*
- *Select appropriate units and tools to measure to the degree of accuracy required in a particular situation*

Measurement
  length
Whole number operations
Ratios
Decimals

Project 2061 Benchmarks
- *Scale drawings show shapes and compare locations of things very different in size.*
- *Use numerical data in describing and comparing objects and events.*

Social Science
Geography

Processes
Observing
Collecting and recording data
Comparing
Working cooperatively
Communicating ideas
Making and reading maps
Formulating questions

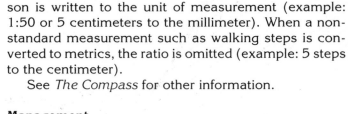

Materials
For each group:
  1 piece of construction paper
  magnetic compasses
  calculator
  Optional: 1 paper fastener

Background Information
The scale format used by The National Geographic Society has been chosen for this book. Where a metric or standard length is used for actual and scale dimen-

sions, a ratio is written first. Then a number comparison is written to the unit of measurement (example: 1:50 or 5 centimeters to the millimeter). When a non-standard measurement such as walking steps is converted to metrics, the ratio is omitted (example: 5 steps to the centimeter).

See *The Compass* for other information.

Management
1. This activity is divided into three parts. In *Part A*, students review the fact sheet and practice using a compass rose. *Part B* involves map reading and creating questions. In *Part C*, students make a playground map. This may take two class periods, one to gather data and one to draw the map. Have groups head to different landmarks or stagger the starting time to keep students from clustering around each landmark.
2. Partners are recommended for all of these activities.
3. Find the declination (see *The Compass*) for your location. Sources include a declination chart, a USGS map, or your shadow. When the sun is directly overhead, your shadow will point to true north. Finding out how much the compass deviates from this shadow is one way to determine declination.
4. To simulate a real map in *Part A*, students can place the compass rose at the top of the sheet. Those who may have difficulty can place the compass rose on the starting point. It may be attached with a paper fastener.
5. A compass is suggested for *Part C* but, once students find north, those who are comfortable with their directions may not need it.
6. A trundle wheel, a piece of string marked in meters, or someone who can take uniform steps are options for measuring distances between landmarks in *Part C*.
7. Data will vary because groups will take different courses to measure landmarks. However, the maps should be similar.

Procedure
Part A
1. Ask the *Key Question*. Then distribute and discuss *The Compass*.
2. Give students *Part A*. Have them cut out the compass rose and place it with north facing in the direction of your choice.
3. Students should record where north points. For example, "North points between B and C" or "North points to K." Up is not always north, so

this provides practice in determining directions whatever the compass orientation.

4. Have students write the cardinal and intermediate initials for points A through L.
5. Choose a new compass position. Have each student rotate their compass rose and repeat the above process.

Part B

6. Distribute the fictional map and questions labeled *Part B*. Have students create and answer their own questions.

Part C

7. Direct a discussion of strategies for completing *Part C.* (use a book or clipboard for writing, agree upon appropriate landmarks that everyone will place on their maps)
8. Have students determine north with a compass adjusted for declination (see *The Compass*).
9. Outside, students should measure distances and determine compass directions for the identified landmarks.
10. Instruct students to determine the scale to be used and figure the scale distance.
11. Have students draw a playground map from the data collected and label the landmarks.
12. Students should brainstorm different ways in which compass directions are used by people in their jobs, hobbies, etc.
13. Guide a concluding discussion.

Discussion

1. Why must you know where north is before you can give compass directions? [All compass directions are based on the position of north.]
2. In what way are compass directions much more accurate than giving directions by saying, "Go left at the tree" or similar directions? [They give a common point of reference.]
3. Give reasons why an airline pilot or ship captain must know compass directions. [lack of landmarks]
4. Why do we always travel in many directions on land before we reach a destination that is in a straight line from us? [Surface routes must be altered because of landforms or water.]
5. In how many ways can compass directions be used? [to give someone specific directions around town, for taking the correct freeway exits or entrances (North Hwy 1, South Hwy 1), to guide airline pilots and ship navigators, to help cross country hikers find their way, to read a map, to guide explorers over land with no landmarks such as Antarctica, to survey land, etc.]

Extensions

1. Bring in a pilot to discuss how directions are found in an airplane.

2. Using road maps, have students give directions from one location to another including compass directions and route.
3. Take a walking tour of the neighborhood or town, following oral and written compass directions. For example, have students give directions from one place of business to another.

Curriculum Correlation

Language Arts

1. Write a report on cartographers or orienteering.
2. Research how the stars were used to guide ships.
3. Write a creative story on the problems Columbus or some other explorer might have had without a compass or the stars.

Art

Create a fictional map. Write questions which require its use.

Technology

Use the interactive program, *Cross-country USA*, by Didatech Software. It integrates the planning of road routes using compass directions, U.S. geography, problem solving, and economics (4th grade and up).

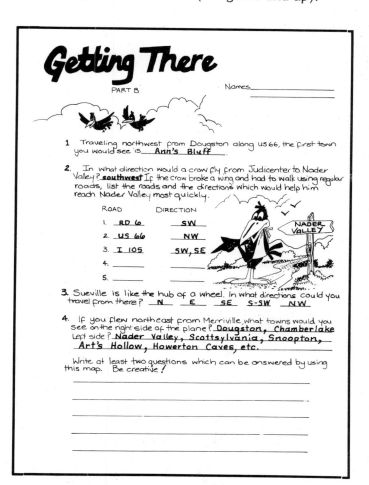

Getting There

Names _____
_____

PART A

1. Cut and place the compass rose on the map as directed. Record the cardinal (N, S, E, W) and intermediate (NE, NW, SE, SW) directions from **START** to each letter.

2. Change the position of the compass rose as directed and repeat.

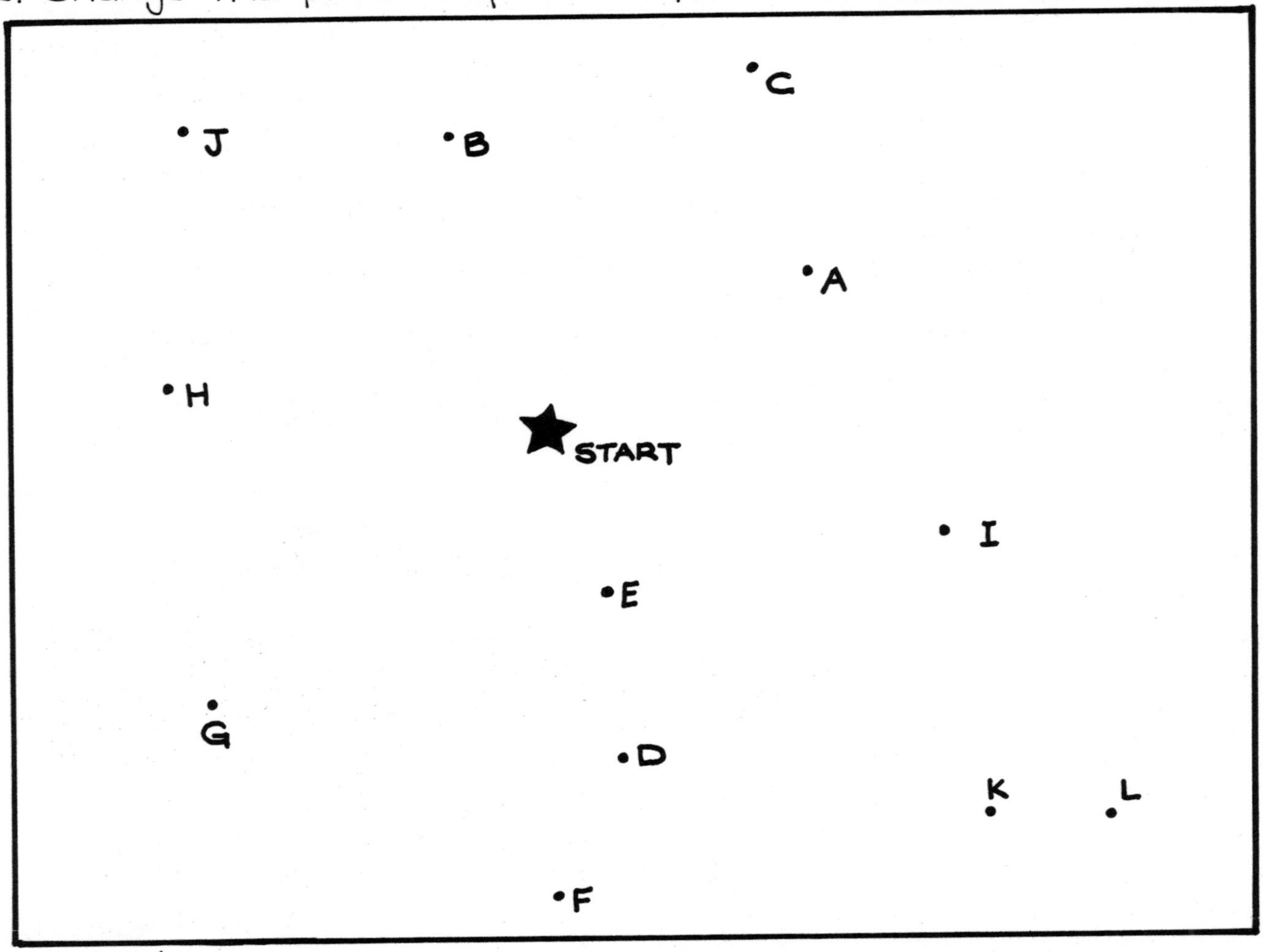

```
                          •C
    •J          •B

                        •A


•H


            ★ START


                      •I
        •E

•G
            •D
                    K    •L
        •F
```

North points_____   North points_____

A_____	G_____	A_____	G_____
B_____	H_____	B_____	H_____
C_____	I_____	C_____	I_____
D_____	J_____	D_____	J_____
E_____	k_____	E_____	K_____
F_____	L_____	F_____	L_____

Getting There

PART B

Names_____
_____

1 Traveling northwest from Dougston along US 66, the first town you would see is_____.

2. In what direction would a crow fly from Judicenter to Nader Valley?_____ If the crow broke a wing and had to walk using regular roads, list the roads and the directions which would help him reach Nader Valley most quickly.

ROAD	DIRECTION
1. _____	_____
2. _____	_____
3. _____	_____
4. _____	_____
5. _____	_____

3. Sueville is like the hub of a wheel. In what directions could you travel from there? _____ _____ _____ _____ _____

4. If you flew northeast from Merriville, what towns would you see on the right side of the plane?_____
Left side?_____
_____

Write at least two questions which can be answered by using this map. Be creative!

_____

_____

_____

_____

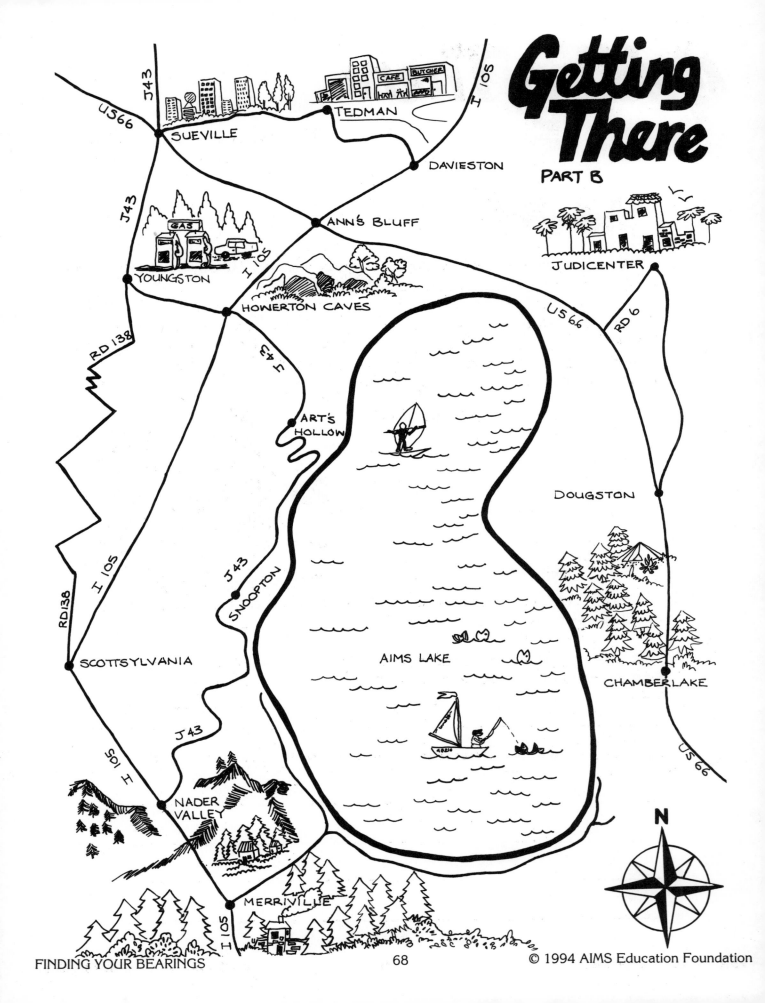

Getting There

PART B

68

Getting There

PART C - PLAYGROUND MAP

1. Determine north with a compass.
2. Start at a corner of your playground. Measure (trundle wheel, string, or walking steps) and record the distance to each landmark. Also record the direction.
3. Decide on a scale.   Example: 5 steps to the cm
4. Draw a map using the information you collected. Label   the landmarks.

EXAMPLE:

SE PLAYGROUND CORNER	TETHERBALL	N W	14 STEPS	2.8 CM

SCALE _____ to the _____cm

FROM	TO	DIRECTION	DISTANCE	SCALE DIST.

Think! In how many ways can compass directions be used ?

_____
_____
_____
_____
_____

THE COMPASS

A compass is a device for determining directions. There are three kinds. The <u>magnetic compass</u> is directed by the earth's magnetism and points to magnetic north. In its simplest form, it is a magnetic needle which turns on a pivot. <u>A gyrocompass</u> is directed by the earth's rotation. It is not affected by magnetism and points to true north. A solar or <u>astrocompass</u> depends on the visible sun or stars. It works in reverse of a sundial.

Several countries claim to have invented the magnetic compass The earliest evidence shows the Chinese used one in 1100, the Western Europeans in 1187, the Arabs in 1220, and the Scandinavians in 1250.

Early ships were wooden so simple magnetic compasses were satisfactory. They usually consisted of a magnetic bar floating in water. Today large ships use a Mariner's compass, a large magnetic compass. A Mariner's compass has several magnets fastened on a flat disk called a compass card. The entire assembly rests on a pivot and is contained in a glass bowl filled with a non-freezable liquid. Since a magnetic compass is affected by the metal used in a ship's construction, adjustments must be made. It is usually used together with a gyrocompass which points to true north.

True or geographical north is what we call the North Pole. Magnetic compasses point to magnetic north which is located near the northern islands of Canada. Magnetic north is determined by the magnetic fields of the earth and moves a few miles from year to year.

The difference between magnetic north and true north at your particular location is called declination and is measured in degrees. It varies from place to place on the earth. To use a magnetic compass accurately, find and set the degree of declination to the right or left of North. In the central Sierra Nevada mountains of California, a magnetic compass should be set to point between 16 and 17 degrees to the right of north. On the East Coast, it will be set a certain number of degrees to the left. United States Geological Survey maps, often used by backpackers, are one source of degrees of declination for your locality.

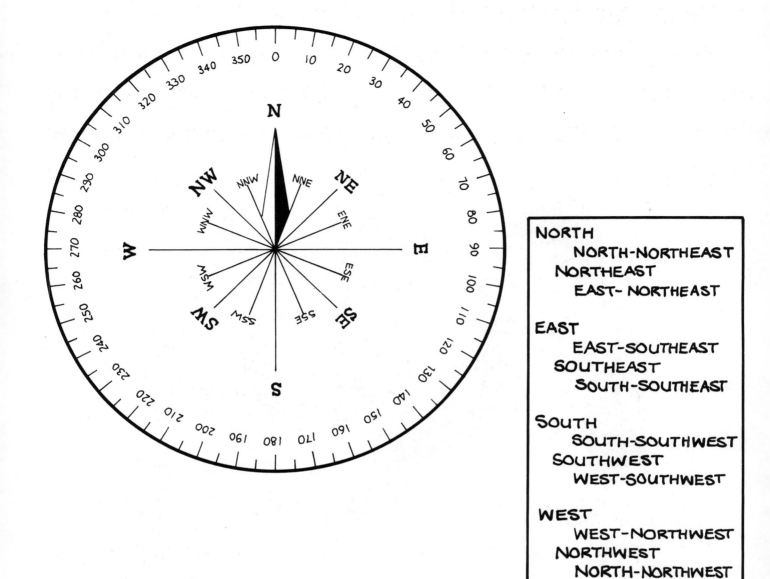

NORTH
    NORTH-NORTHEAST
NORTHEAST
    EAST- NORTHEAST

EAST
    EAST-SOUTHEAST
SOUTHEAST
    SOUTH-SOUTHEAST

SOUTH
    SOUTH-SOUTHWEST
SOUTHWEST
    WEST-SOUTHWEST

WEST
    WEST-NORTHWEST
NORTHWEST
    NORTH-NORTHWEST

Boxing the compass refers to naming the 32 points marked on the compass face. Modern magnetic compasses are marked with the 16 main points shown above as well as the 360 degrees of a circle. North is at 0°, east at 90°, south at 180°, and west at 270°. North, south, east and west are called cardinal points. Intercardinal or intermediate points are northeast, northwest, southeast, and southwest.

Fire on the Mountain

Topic
Fire lookout simulation

Key Question
How can a compass locate fires, assist campers, and save lives?

Focus
Students will use compasses to locate points on a map and solve problems typical of those a forest service lookout may have.

Math
NCTM Standards
- *Use mathematics in other curriculum areas*
- *Estimate, make, and use measurements to describe and compare phenomena*

Estimation
Measurement
    angle
    length
Whole number operations
Problem solving

Project 2061 Benchmarks
- *In making decisions, it helps to take time to consider the benefits and drawbacks of alternatives.*
- *It takes two numbers to locate a point on a map or any other flat surface. The numbers may be two perpendicular distances from a point, or an angle and a distance from a point.*
- *Models are often used to think about processes that happen too slowly, too quickly, or on too small a scale to observe directly, or that are too vast to be changed deliberately, or that are potentially dangerous.*
- *Estimate distances and travel times from maps and the actual size of objects from scale drawings.*

Social Science
Geography

Processes
Observing
Collecting and recording data
Comparing
Identifying variables
Interpreting data
Generalizing
Applying

Working cooperatively
Communicating ideas
Reading maps
Considering multiple points of view

Materials
Metric rulers

Background Information
The ability to determine direction and distance are two key skills that a forest service lookout must have to protect the lives of many people and sometimes thousands of acres of land. Towers are equipped with fire finders (azimuths), telephones, short wave radios, and binoculars. The lookout, after seeing suspicious smoke, will contact another forest service tower to see if they can confirm the smoke and help pinpoint the exact location. Airplanes and people living in the area may also be contacted to confirm a possible fire.

How is the location of the fire determined? Two lookout towers each measure the direction of the fire with the compass degrees on their fire finder. A line extending from that angle on a map will intersect with one from the other tower, pinpointing the location of the suspected fire. Then the appropriate support personnel can be notified. Aside from distance and direction, variables such as firefighter location, mountain elevations, and non-threatening smoke will call upon the problem solving and logical thinking skills of the persons working on this simulation.

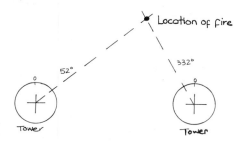

Management
1. Groups of two or three work well. Jobs might include a lookout (reads scenario), a fireboss (locates smoke position on map), and a commander (keeps crew on task, records answers, and directs discussion).
2. Studying background information, reviewing compass and protractor skills, and completing the *Training Sheet* can be done in one class period. The *Daily Log* will take another period.
3. Preliminary experience in reading protractors is recommended.

4. The towers are located at the center intersection of the compasses. Always measure degrees and distances from this point.
5. Small squares on the map help pinpoint building locations for the *Fire Lookout Training Sheet*. Decisions will have to be made about where to measure at lakes and mountains, a good point for class discussion. The lake edge or mountain base nearest the tower might be considered. Due to possible variations, the answer key is only a guide.
6. When locating a fire, encourage students to place two straight edges in position to find the intersection. Mark with a dot or an X.

Procedure
1. Divide the class into groups and ask the *Key Question*.
2. Present the problem of detecting forest fires from a lookout station. Use the *Background Information* or have students research their own.
3. Distribute the map and have students study it. Point out the distance scale and mountain elevations.
4. Have students practice using the map and the compass/protractor by completing the *Fire Lookout Training Sheet*.
5. Give students the *Scenario*; have them read it carefully.
6. Distribute the *Daily Log* and instruct students to solve the problems it presents.
7. Have the groups share the decisions they made and discuss questions.

Discussion
1. What is the most difficult part of a fire lookout's job? [being alone for long periods of time]
2. Why is teamwork necessary to be a good lookout? [so you can locate a fire by triangulation]
3. Is the human element necessary to be a lookout, or could lookouts be replaced by machines? [People are necessary because visual observation, interpretation of smoke, and decision-making are not within the realm of artificial intelligence given to machines. Today, however, fire detection personnel are increasingly found in aircraft with locational and infrared equipment rather than in a lookout tower.]
4. Discuss where each group would locate the new Crystal Point Lookout. Evaluate their reasons. (Consider surrounding elevations, distance from other lookout, etc.)

Extensions
1. Invite a forest service lookout to describe the job.
2. If your school is located near a national forest, visit a lookout station on a field trip.

Curriculum Correlation
Language Arts
1. Research the history of fire lookout stations.
2. Use the map to continue writing the *Daily Log* through the month of June.
3. Use actual forest service maps to set up a new scenario.
4. Design a different forest service map and write scenarios for classmates to solve.

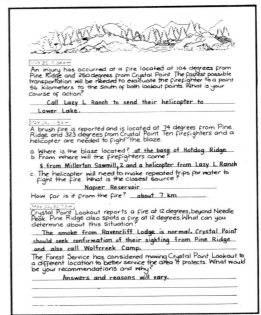

74

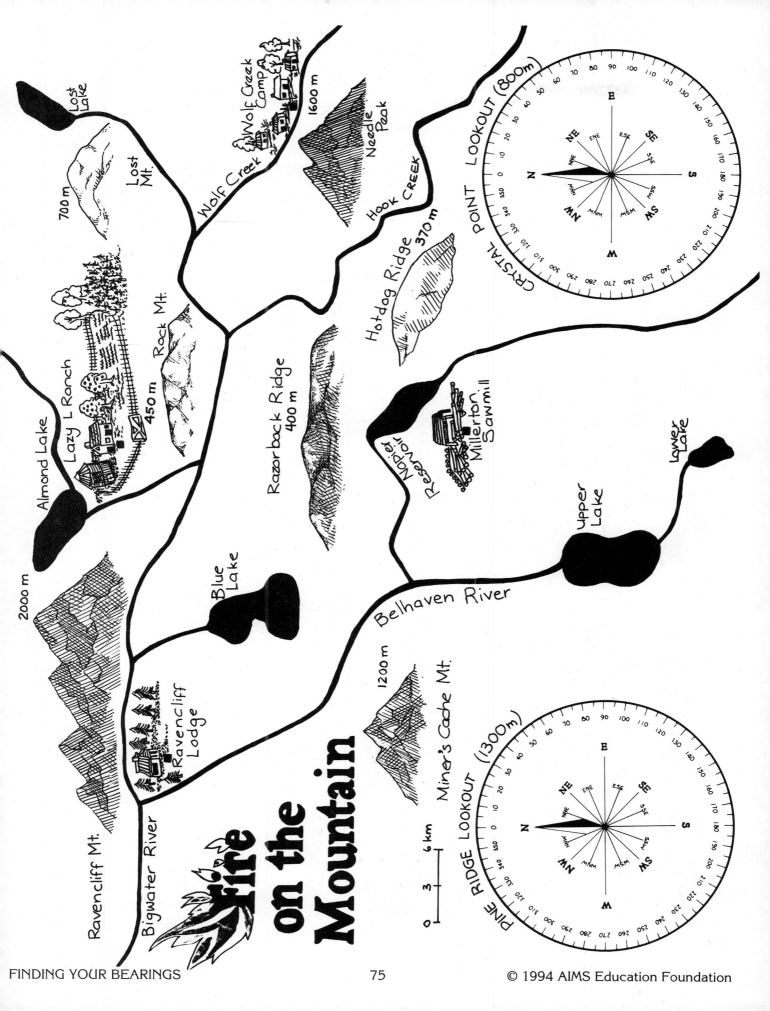

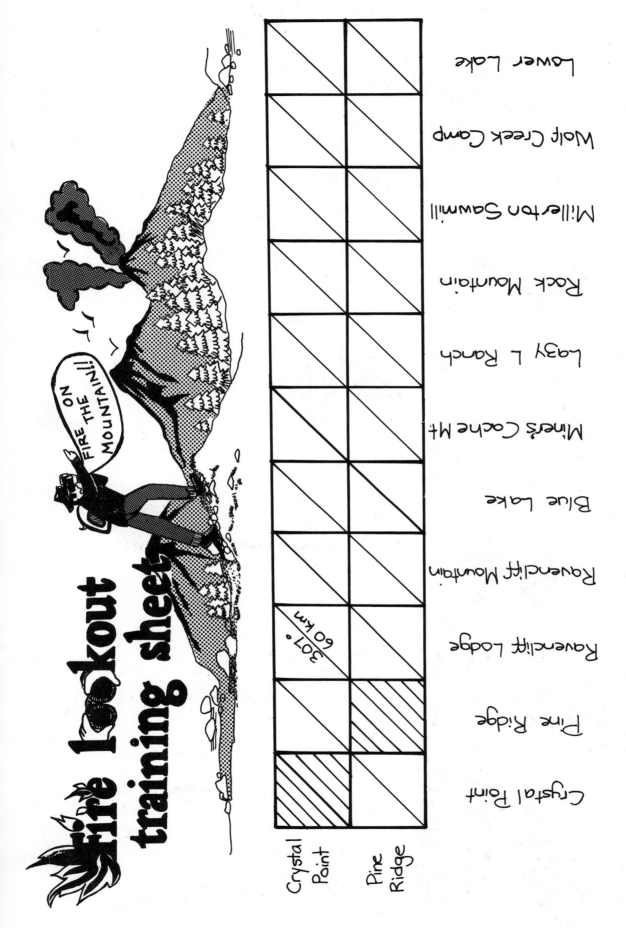

Fire lookout training sheet

Directions:

Match locations on the chart and give compass degrees and distance by using the map.

	Crystal Point	Pine Ridge	Ravencliff Lodge	Ravencliff Mountain	Blue Lake	Miner's Cache Mt.	Lazy L Ranch	Rock Mountain	Millerton Sawmill	Wolf Creek Camp	Lower Lake
Crystal Point		307° 60 km									
Pine Ridge											

Fire on the Mountain

You are a team of fire lookouts assigned to two different locations in the national forest. Part of your team will be at Pine Ridge Lookout and the other part at the Crystal Point Lookout Station. Both stations work together to spot fires, determine their severity, and alert necessary fire crews. Posted on the wall of each lookout station is a set of instructions listing available help and their locations.

Instructions

1. Ravencliff Lodge will have smoke billowing from a cooking fireplace. Four staff members are volunteer firefighters.
2. Miner's Cache Mountain has occasional campers and, as a result, some campfire smoke may be noted. There are no available firefighters in the area.
3. Millerton Sawmill will have a steady plume of smoke from their chip operation. There are eight available firefighters.
4. Wolfcreek Camp should be called if any smoke north of Needle Peak is noticed. A three-person fire crew and canoes are available.
5. Lazy L Ranch has eight people available for firefighting and a helicopter able to transport four people.
6. The distance between lookout stations is 56 kilometers.

Daily Log
Fire on the Mountain

MAY 7, 10:25 am.
Fire breaks out on the highest point of Razorback Ridge. What are the compass readings from each lookout station?

_____

MAY 7, 1:07 p.m.
Pine Ridge Lookout spots smoke at 55 degrees and at a distance of about 70 kilometers. Crystal Point cannot make the same spotting. What could be a reason for this and what should be done?

_____
_____

MAY 7, 2:34 p.m.
Pine Ridge spots a fire at 20 degrees and Crystal Point at 291 degrees. What is the location of the fire?

_____
_____

MAY 11, 4:31 p.m.
Fire is spotted at the easternmost point of Rock Mountain.
   a. What is the compass reading for each lookout station?

_____

   b. What is the closest lookout station?_____
      What is the air distance between the closest lookout
      station and the fire?_____
   c. Six people are needed to fight the fire. From where should
      they be dispatched?

_____

MAY 19, 8:34 a.m.
A concerned camper at Rock Mountain radios in about a column of smoke he sees due south. Pine Ridge plots it at 68 degrees, Crystal Point at 304 degrees. What will their report say?

_____
_____

78

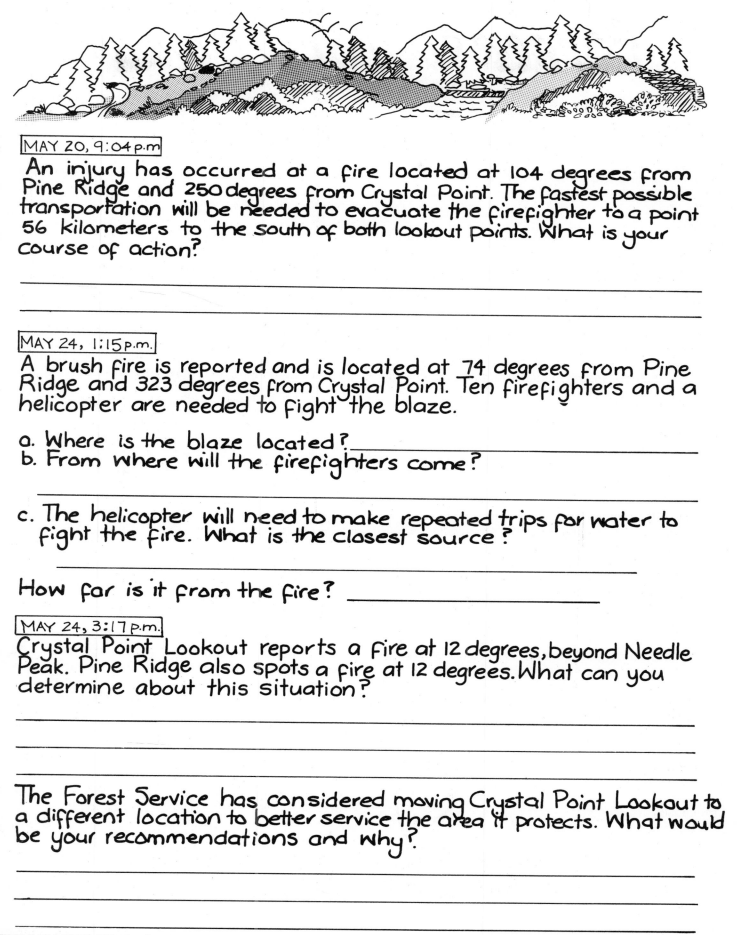

MAY 20, 9:04 p.m.

An injury has occurred at a fire located at 104 degrees from Pine Ridge and 250 degrees from Crystal Point. The fastest possible transportation will be needed to evacuate the firefighter to a point 56 kilometers to the south of both lookout points. What is your course of action?

_____

_____

MAY 24, 1:15 p.m.

A brush fire is reported and is located at 74 degrees from Pine Ridge and 323 degrees from Crystal Point. Ten firefighters and a helicopter are needed to fight the blaze.

a. Where is the blaze located? _____

b. From where will the firefighters come?

_____

c. The helicopter will need to make repeated trips for water to fight the fire. What is the closest source?

_____

How far is it from the fire? _____

MAY 24, 3:17 p.m.

Crystal Point Lookout reports a fire at 12 degrees, beyond Needle Peak. Pine Ridge also spots a fire at 12 degrees. What can you determine about this situation?

_____

_____

The Forest Service has considered moving Crystal Point Lookout to a different location to better service the area it protects. What would be your recommendations and why?

_____

_____

_____

Forecast for Today

Topic
Temperature patterns

Key Question
You are planning a trip to another city. How will you decide what clothes to pack?

Focus
Students will use newspaper weather reports or other resources to examine the temperature patterns of their chosen city for one week.

Math
NCTM Standards
- *Systematically collect, organize, and describe data*
- *Construct, read, and intepret displays of data*
- *Select and use an appropriate method for computing from among mental arithmetic, paper-and-pencil, calculator, and computer methods*

Whole number operations
Statistics
    mean
Graphs
    line
    bar

Project 2061 Benchmarks
- *The graphic display of numbers may help to show patterns such as trends, varying rates of change, gaps, or clusters. Such patterns sometimes can be used to make predictions about the phenomena being graphed.*
- *Physical and biological systems tend to change until they become stable and then remain that way unless their surroundings change.*
- *Locate information in reference books, back issues of newspapers and magazines, compact disks, and computer databases.*

Social Science
Geography

Science
Meteorology

Processes
Predicting
Observing
Collecting and recording data
Comparing
Interpreting data
Inferring

Generalizing
Applying

Materials
Newspaper weather reports or alternate source, one per student or group
Colored pencils or crayons

Background Information
Most newspapers feature a daily weather report with high and low temperature readings for major cities in the state, the nation, and the world. A national weather map also shows warm and cold fronts, rain, snow, etc. Other sources of weather information such as cable television or telecommunication networks may be available.

This activity may be done with either Celsius or Fahrenheit measurements depending on the availability of such information. Do not have students convert Fahrenheit to Celsius.

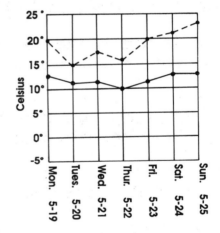

To make a line graph, first identify the lowest and highest numbers to be recorded. Temperatures below zero mean that negative numbers, zero, and positive numbers are needed on the graph. The size of the increments (1's, 2's, 5's, 10's...) depends on the temperature range. Use small increments for a small range, larger increments for a wide range. Label the bottom and side of the graph and record each temperature with a point. Using different colors or kinds of lines, connect the high temperature points with one line and the low temperature points with another. Decide on a graph title.

Management
(Following are two different approaches for presenting this lesson in addition to the usual *Procedure*. These are offered for those teachers whose students are prepared for more independent investigations.)

1. Daily newspaper weather reports can be brought in by students and duplicated, if more are needed. It is helpful to enlarge the small print.
2. Saturday and Sunday information needs to be obtained from the weekend preceding or concluding the activity.
3. Decide from which list (state, national, world) students will choose cities. For example, a class studying U.S. history might want to choose U. S. cities.
4. Students may work individually or with a partner.
5. The initial activity will take about 30 minutes. Then allow 5-10 minutes per day to record temperatures. The concluding computation, graphing, and discussion will take about 40 minutes. Another period should be spent comparing the temperature ranges for ten cities.
6. The number recorded in the temperature range column should be the difference between the high and low temperature.

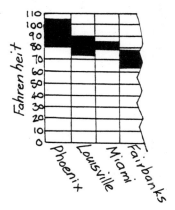

7. The average temperature range graph should be constructed by marking the average high and low temperatures for each city and coloring the band between the two marks.

Procedure
1. Ask the *Key Question*. Focus on the importance of weather in making such a decision.

2. Introduce students to the features of a newspaper weather report or whatever source is being used. Ask, "Is the temperature listed in Celsius or Fahrenheit?"
3. Give students the first activity sheet. Have them pick a city and predict its average high and low temperatures for the coming week.
4. Students should research and record the physical geography of the city's location sometime during the week.
5. Direct students to record their city's high and low for seven days.
6. Have students compute the average high and low temperatures and temperature range.
7. Distribute the *Line Graph* and have students construct the graph and key, using different colors for the daily high and low temperatures (see *Background Information*).
8. Lead a class discussion. Compare results and decide what clothes would be needed for each city.
9. Give students the *Average Temperature Range* sheet. Students should compare the average temperature range of ten cities from class data. Ask them to write a specific number of inferences based on the graph and map study. Discuss possible reasons for temperature range variations.

Discussion
1. What clothes would you take if you were traveling to your chosen city?
2. Which city had the highest average temperature this week? ...the lowest?
3. Which day had the widest temperature range?
4. Was your temperature range close together or far apart? Why?
5. Predict the temperature in your city for next week. What might cause it to change from last week? [a change in air pressure systems, the movement of warm/cold fronts, etc.]
6. How does the geography of a region help determine a city's weather pattern? [The presence of water makes it humid, deserts are hot and dry, mountains surrounding a valley reduce air movement, higher elevations are generally cooler, etc.]
7. Compare the temperature of your chosen city with that of your home town.

Average Temperature Range Graph
8. What statements can be made based on the graph?
9. Which cities differ by about ten degrees?
10. What might cause the differences in average temperature ranges? [geography, high and low pressure system patterns, etc.]

Extensions
1. Enlarge a state, national, or world map and have students show the average highs or lows for their city. Together, devise a key depicting temperature ranges. Students can draw the appropriate symbol

or color for their city on a rectangle or circle and glue it on the map. Use for discussion.

2. Do a year-long study of world temperatures by picking six cities from each of the major continents. A variety of coastal and inland cities should be chosen. On the *Monthly Temperatures* sheet, record the temperature range for a certain day each month (September 5, October 5, …) for up to twelve months. Current data as well as data from back issues of the newspaper may be used. Write conclusions about the data.

3. Research Celsius and Fahrenheit.

4. Have the students staple the weeks' newspaper weather maps in order and then flip through them to see a visual movement of weather.

Curriculum Correlation

Language Arts

Write a weather bulletin or forecast for the day or week and read as a television report. Have several students do one each day.

Science

For other activities related to weather, see the AIMS books, *Overhead and Underfoot* and *Down to Earth*.

Forecast for Today

_____

_____ Names

City _____

Physical geography _____

_____

_____

Predicted average high temperature _____

Predicted average low temperature _____

Record the daily high and low temperatures for your city.

DATE	DAY	TEMPERATURE		
		HIGH	LOW	RANGE
TOTAL				
AVERAGE				

If you were visiting this city tomorrow, what kinds of clothes would you pack?

_____

_____

Forecast for Today

LINE GRAPH

Title

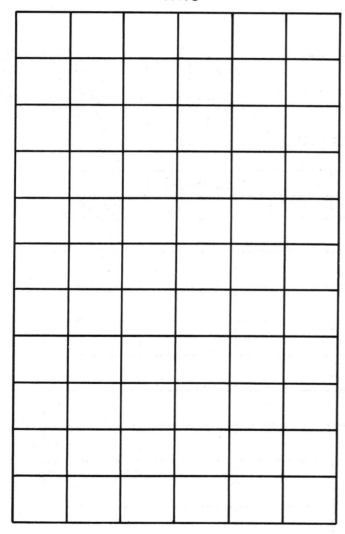

KEY

Forecast for Today

Name _____

Average Temperature Range for _____
(week)

Collect information from other groups and record the average temperature range for ten cities during one week.

Write two or more statements from the information on the graph.

_____

_____

_____

_____

_____

85

Name _____

Forecast for Today

MONTHLY TEMPERATURES

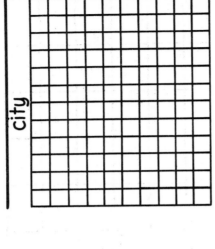

city

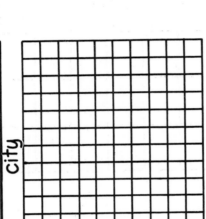

city

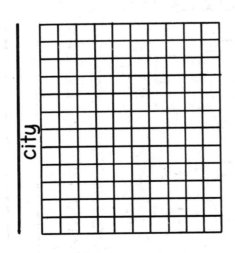

city

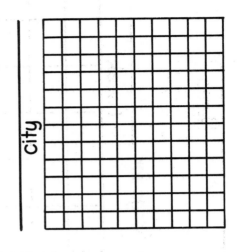

city

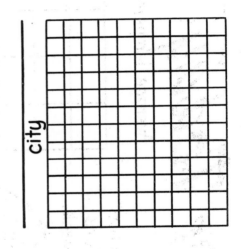

city

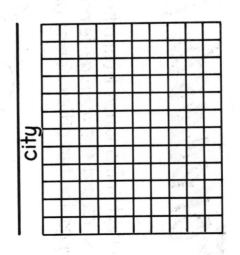

city

Count me in!

Topic
Taking a census

Key Questions
1. How can a person estimate large numbers without actually counting them?
2. How is it possible to count how many people there are in the world?

Focus
Students will use a random sample to determine the population of a given area.

Math
NCTM Standards
- *Explore problems and describe results using graphical, numerical, physical, algebraic, and verbal mathematical models or representations*
- *Make inferences and convincing arguments that are based on data analysis*

Count
Measurement
   length
Whole number operations
Formulas
   area
Statistics
   random sampling
   mean

Project 2061 Benchmarks
- *A small part of something may be special in some way and not give an accurate picture of the whole. How much a portion of something can help to estimate what the whole is like depends on how the portion is chosen. There is a danger of choosing only the data that show what is expected by the person doing the choosing.*
- *Be skeptical of arguments based on very small samples of data, biased samples, or samples for which there was no control sample.*

Social Science
Geography
   population

Processes
Observing
Collecting and recording data
Comparing
Controlling variables
Interpreting data
Inferring
Generalizing
Working cooperatively
Communicating ideas

Materials
Two 1 lb. bags of lima beans
40 meters of string
4 meter length of string, 1 per group
Meter sticks, long meter tape, or trundle wheel
Watch or clock that can measure seconds
Optional: calculators

Background Information
See *Taking a Census* and *Random Sampling*.

Management
1. Plan at least one hour for discussion of the concept and the activity. Final discussion and applications will depend on the needs of the class.
2. Groups of four or five are recommended. One person should be the group walker and the remaining team members will use string to outline the sample area and count the beans within it. Each team member should be responsible for recording the data at least once.
3. Time should be allowed to discuss the findings of the sampling activity and its impact on census taking, polls, etc.
4. Outline the census area, preferably grass, with string or pylons before students arrive. A 10 x 10 meter area is easiest mathematically, but other square or rectangular measurements may be used. Distribute all of the beans over the area in a random manner. Don't forget the corners!

Procedure
1. Set up the problem of census taking by asking one of the *Key Questions*. Allow students to make guesses as to how a census or opinion poll is conducted.
2. Have students cut a 4-meter length of string and mark each meter.
3. Students should measure and record the length and width of the census area to determine the total area.
4. Instruct student groups to stand around the perimeter of the census area and each send one walker to the middle of the area.
5. Direct the walkers to walk aimlessly about the area. They must stay inside the boundaries and

not walk with another person. Walking with closed eyes may help the sample be truly random, but another team member should help the walker avoid bumping others.

6. Tell the walkers to stop and freeze after 30 seconds.
7. Student groups should go to their walker and outline a square meter at the walker's right foot with the 4-meter string. The meter marks identify the corners.

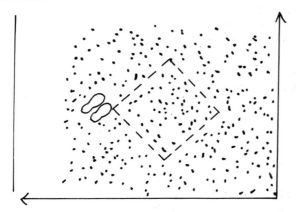

8. Two or three group members should count the beans in the sample area. The remaining team member should record the data.
9. Repeat steps five through eight two more times.
10. Have students clean the area by picking up the beans and boundary markers. This may be done after the class discussion, if desired.
11. Students should find the total, average, and projected population based on their samples.

Average x (Total Area/Area of Sample) = Projected Population

12. Have the groups report their results to the class so the data can be recorded in the table and compared. If more math practice is desired, groups can report their samples and everyone figure the total, average, and projected total population for all groups.
13. Lead a discussion on the accuracy and problems with this method of census taking.

Discussion

1. What are some positive points about a random sample census? [quick, easy, relatively accurate] Negative? [not 100% accurate]
2. How do your results compare with other group results?
3. What are some factors that may have led to inaccuracies in our random sample? [how evenly the beans were dispersed, beans overlooked because of the height of the grass, etc.]
4. How are some of the difficulties we experienced similar to real problems in a random sample? For example, if some beans were hidden by tall grass, could that be related to the problem of finding every residence in a rural or urban area? [Problems that surfaced in the 1990 U.S. census, which attempted to count every person, were lack of cooperation, illiteracy, language, and finding the homeless or those with no mail address.]
5. Why was it necessary to choose three samples in the one area and find an average? [The more samples, the more accurate the results.]

Extensions

1. Invite a pollster to class to explain the process of polling the general public.
2. Gather examples of polls published in such sources as news magazines. Make note of the sampling error.

Curriculum Correlation

Language Arts

Design an opinion poll questionnaire about some subject of interest such as favorite pastime activities at your school. Use random sampling to compile statistics.

Technology

Make and use a survey with a computer program such as *Survey Taker* from Scholastic.

Count me in!

Group — Names:

_____

_____

_____

_____

Area of sample: _____ m²

Total area of population: _____ x _____ = _____ m²

SAMPLE	GROUP RESULTS							
	A	B	C	D	E	F	G	H
1								
2								
3								
TOTAL								
AVERAGE								
PROJECTED TOTAL POPULATION								

Using your group's average, determine the population of the total area.

_____ x _____ = _____

How do your results compare with other group results?

_____

_____

Taking a Census

A census is a survey conducted by a nation's government to gather information about its people. At least 90% of the world's nations conduct some kind of census. Some countries only conduct a population census. Others, like the United States, conduct a census with many questions. Information gathered in a census may include population, housing, agriculture, government, construction, manufacturing, mineral industries, and transportation. Other information gathered about the general population may include age, employment, income, sex and race.

The first American census was taken in 1790. The enumerators, people who did the actual counting, surveyed the country on horseback. It took 18 months to count the nearly four million people then living in the U.S. Taxes and congressional representation were determined from this information.

The way a census is conducted depends on the information that needs to be gathered. For a population census, the Census Bureau tries to reach every household. For other types, the Bureau surveys a representative sample. Every fourth or fifth home may be contacted about certain information and the results will be adjusted to apply to the entire population.

Some nations with expansive unpopulated areas will use a representative sample to determine the population of the entire area. A large area is divided into smaller regions. Then specific regions are chosen by chance and every person in the region is questioned. The results are multiplied by the number of regions in the area to determine a total number.

Random Sampling

In addition to a census, random sampling is often used for opinion polls. The topic of an opinion poll might be how people feel about a Presidential candidate or current world, national, or local issues.

Two rules must be followed to obtain a random sample. 1) The size of the sample must be large enough to show reliable results. 2) The sample must be random; all members of the population must have an equal chance of being chosen.

Every random sample has a sampling error, found with special formulas, which determines its accuracy. For example, if a sample produces an estimated population of 1,367 and the sampling error is plus or minus 5, the actual population could be between 1,299 and 1,435. The actual results could be as much as 5% more or less than those given. The greater the sampling error, the less accurate the results.

Topic
World population trends

Key Question
How fast is the world growing?

Focus
Students will examine four decades of population data on the eleven most populous countries of the world and project their future growth.

Math
NCTM Standards
- *Select and use an appropriate method for computing from among mental arithmetic, paper-and-pencil, calculator, and computer methods*
- *Construct, read, and interpret displays of data*
- *Make inferences and convincing arguments that are based on data analysis*

Estimation
  rounding
Whole number operations
Statistics
Order
Graphs

Project 2061 Benchmarks
- *The graphic display of numbers may help to show patterns such as trends, varying rates of change, gaps, or clusters. Such patterns sometimes can be used to make predictions about the phenomena being graphed.*
- *The global environment is affected by national policies and practices relating to energy use, waste disposal, ecological management, manufacturing, and population.*

Social Science
Geography
Ethics

Processes
Predicting
Observing
Comparing
Interpreting data
Inferring
Working cooperatively
Communicating ideas
Making and reading maps
Considering multiple points of view
Appreciating rights and responsibilities

Materials
World maps in textbooks/atlases
Calculators
Colored pencils
Straight edges

Background Information
The subject of population trends can branch in many directions. This is a structured activity focusing on the world's most populated countries. An open-ended version, *People 'Plosion II*, follows.

We are an international community, numbering over five billion people. Because of our interdependence and the shrinking of natural resources, the population trends of the world are becoming increasingly important. Some of the issues raised involve moral and ethical considerations. The People's Republic of China, the most highly populated country in the world, has mandated that parents have only one child. The laws are set up to favor those who comply and discriminate against those who don't. Possible solutions to the world's problem need to be addressed by the generation now being trained.

It should be noted that the population of Pakistan decreased between 1969 and 1979. The cause of this was the 1971 split of West and East Pakistan, after a nine-month civil war, into two countries: Pakistan (formerly West Pakistan) and Bangladesh (formerly East Pakistan).

The U.S.S.R. split into several countries in 1991, making projections more difficult to verify.

Management
1. Students should work in pairs.
2. This activity may be divided into three parts: 1) map 2) line graph and projected population and 3) density, ranking, and discussion.

Procedure
1. Ask the *Key Question*.
2. Have student pairs locate, color, and label the listed eleven countries on the world map.
3. Students should glue the line graph together and plot the population data on it. They should use a different color for each country and label the lines.
4. Have students estimate the projected populations visually by continuing the lines on the graph to 2009. They should be prepared to give the rationale for the way they drew the slope.
5. Direct students to record the projected populations based on the lines they drew.
6. Students should compute the population density for each country.

7. Have students rank the countries by population and density.
8. Discuss the implications of the results.

Discussion
1. Why did you draw the projected population lines the way you did? [used an average slope, used the slope between 1979 and 1989]
2. What factors change the population? [births, deaths, immigration]
3. Does past growth guarantee future growth? Why or why not?
4. Which continent appears to have the greatest share of the world's population? [Asia]
5. Which country has been growing the fastest?
6. Which was the decade of greatest growth for _____ ?
7. Has the rate of growth been fast or slow for _____ ?
8. How does density affect living conditions?
9. Why should we be concerned about population trends of the world? [world's resources, poverty, pollution, jobs, etc.] Is more better?

10. What solutions can you offer to solve the world's population problems? Do you agree with China's approach? Why or why not?

Extensions
1. Select three countries and write about the pattern of growth over four decades.
2. Figure the percent of growth each decade for each country.
3. Write to **The World Bank, 1818 H. Street, N.W., Washington, D.C. 20433** for the current *The World Bank Atlas*. It is filled with economic maps, life expectancy maps, etc.

Curriculum Correlation
Math

Use a trundle wheel to measure a square kilometer in your community. Link to a discussion of density.

People Plosion I

Names ______________________

____

Color and label the eleven most populated countries in the world.

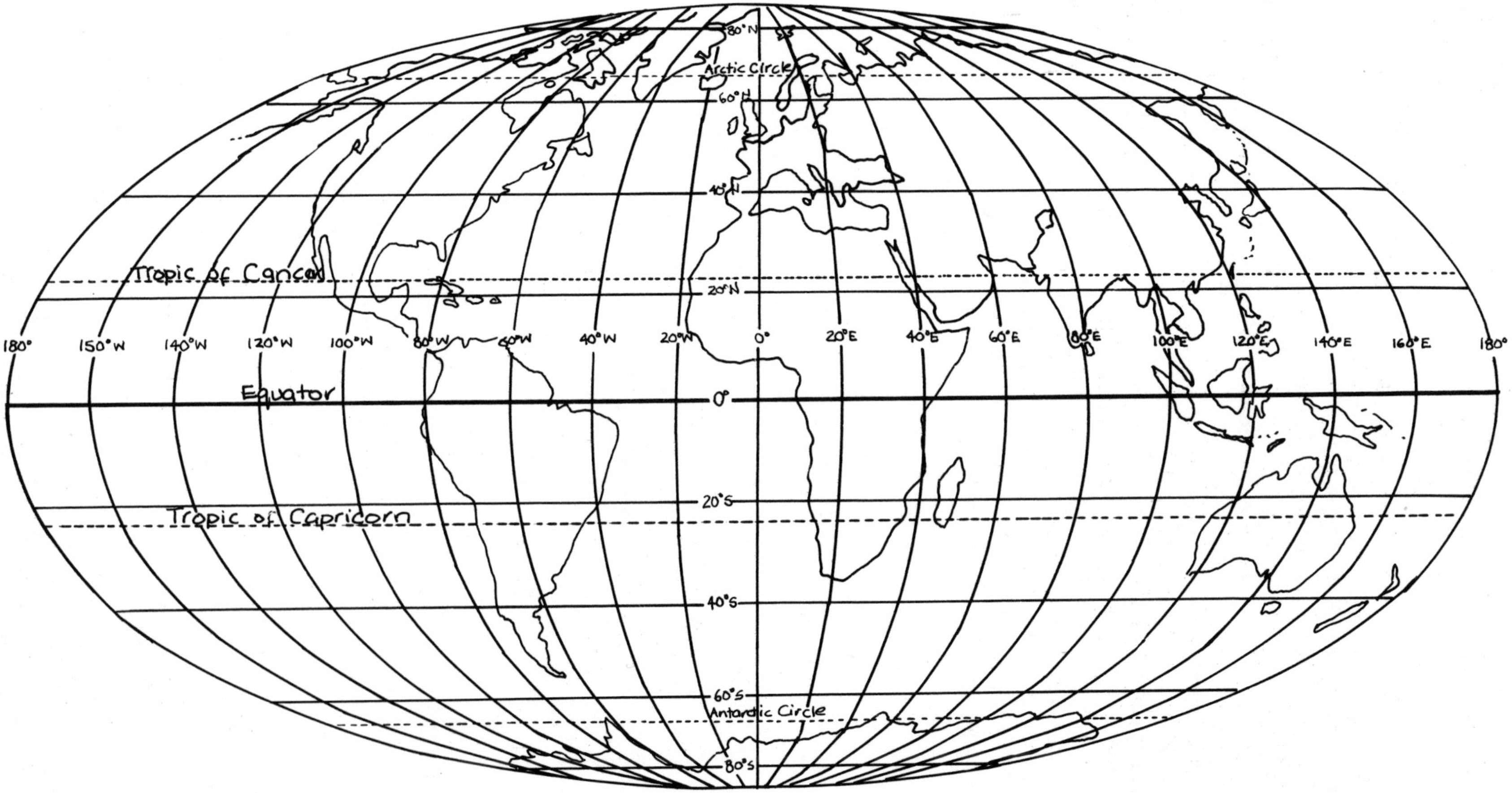
80°N
Arctic Circle
60°N
40°N
Tropic of Cancer
20°N
180°
150°W
140°W
120°W
100°W
80°W
60°W
40°W
20°W
0°
20°E
40°E
60°E
80°E
100°E
120°E
140°E
160°E
180°
Equator
0°
20°S
Tropic of Capricorn
40°S
60°S
Antarctic Circle
80°S

Using the statistics and this map, which continent shows the greatest population?

____

Names _____

People Explosion I

THE WORLD'S MOST POPULATED COUNTRIES

COUNTRY	1959*	1969*	1979*	1989*	PROJECTED POPULATION**	
					1999	2009
Bangladesh	—	—	88,092,000	112,757,000		
Brazil	68,000,000	93,700,000	119,175,000	153,992,000		
China (People's Republic)	669,000,000	740,000,000	1,012,197,000	1,069,628,000		
India	402,750,000	536,938,000	667,326,000	833,422,000		
Indonesia	89,600,000	116,000,000	148,085,000	187,726,000		
Japan	92,740,000	102,322,000	115,880,000	123,231,000		
Mexico	34,625,903	48,313,438	65,770,000	88,087,000		
Nigeria	35,000,000	63,870,000	74,595,000	115,152,000		
Pakistan	88,211,000	132,000,000	84,075,000	110,358,000		
U.S.S.R.	208,826,000	241,748,000	262,436,000	287,015,000		
United States	179,323,175	200,255,151	222,020,000	247,498,000		

* The World Almanac and Book of Facts 1961, 1971, 1981, 1989. (estimates and census figures.)

** Transfer estimates from line graph.

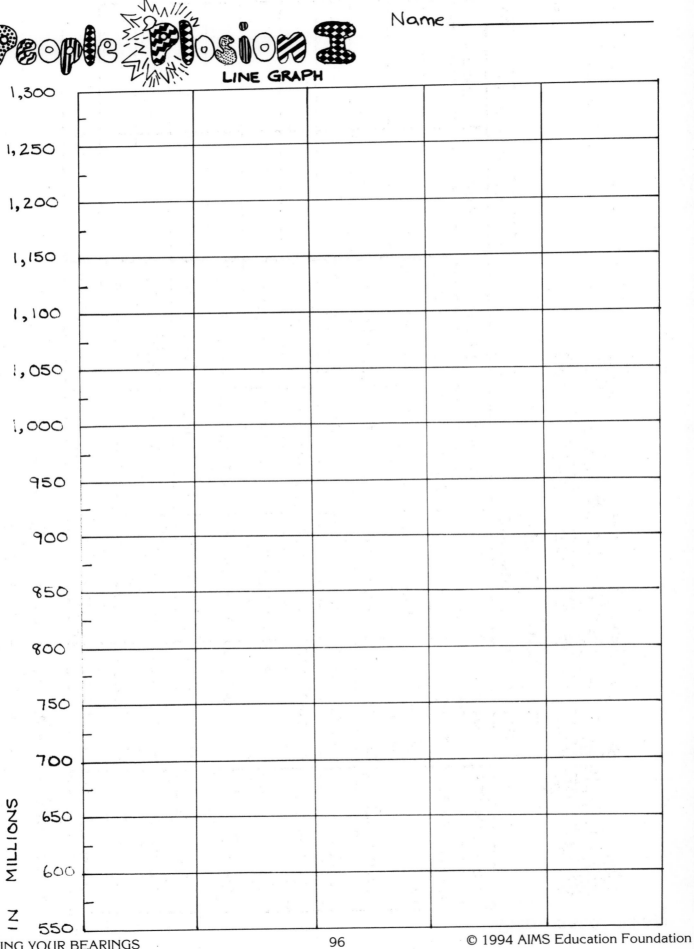

People Plosion I

LINE GRAPH

Name _____

IN MILLIONS

1,300
1,250
1,200
1,150
1,100
1,050
1,000
950
900
850
800
750
700
650
600
550

Cut and glue to rest of graph.

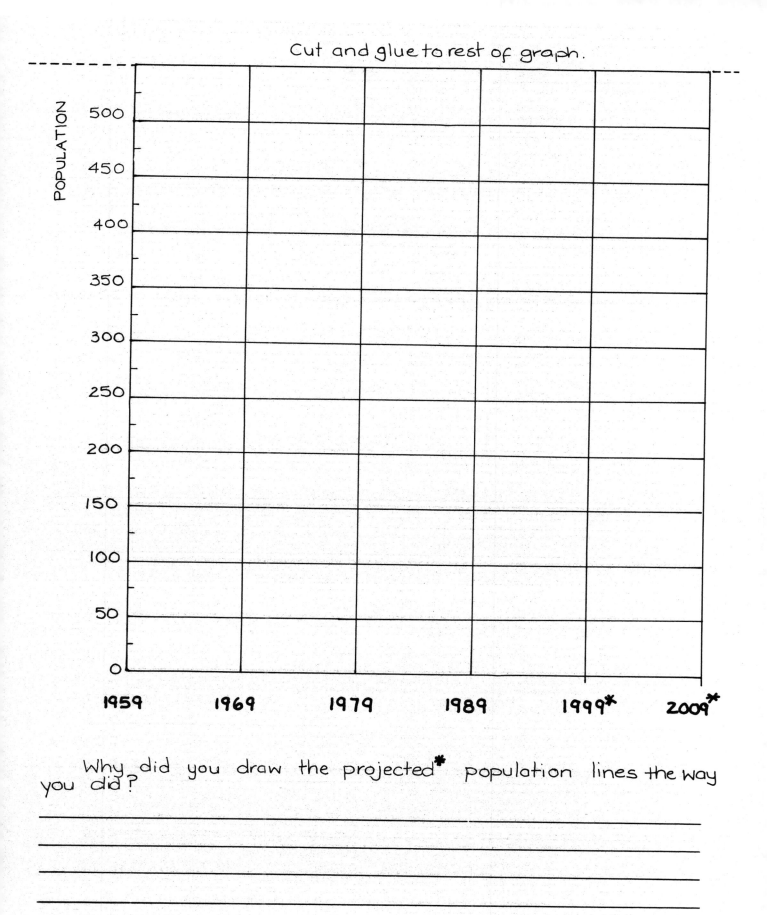

POPULATION

500

450

400

350

300

250

200

150

100

50

0

1959   1969   1979   1989   1999*   2009*

Why did you draw the projected* population lines the way you did?

_____

_____

_____

_____

Record your estimated numbers for 1999 and 2009 on the population table.

People Plosion I
DENSITY

Names _____

_____

Density is the average number of people concentrated in a certain amount of space.

COUNTRY	1989 POPULATION*	AREA* (km²)	DENSITY**
Bangladesh	112,757,000	89,457	
Brazil	153,992,000	5,287,930	
China (People's Republic)	1,069,628,000	5,961,973	
India	833,422,000	2,037,951	
Indonesia	187,726,000	1,183,046	
Japan	123,231,000	234,682	
Mexico	88,087,000	1,225,421	
Nigeria	115,152,000	573,877	
Pakistan	110,358,000	499,438	
U.S.S.R.	287,015,000	13,917,039	
United States	247,498,000	5,822,601	

*The World Almanac and Book of Facts 1989
(area figures converted from sq. miles to sq. km)

**Population ÷ Area (Because of calculator limitations, figure as in the example for Bangladesh: 112,757 ÷ 89.457)

Rank the above countries by:

POPULATION

1. _____
2. _____
3. _____
4. _____
5. _____
6. _____
7. _____
8. _____
9. _____
10. _____
11. _____

DENSITY

1. _____
2. _____
3. _____
4. _____
5. _____
6. _____
7. _____
8. _____
9. _____
10. _____
11. _____

People Plosion II

Topic
Population trends (open-ended)

Key Question
What are the population trends in _____ ?
(state, country, or world)

Focus
Students will research past, present, and compute future population trends in the most highly populated locations in the world, country, or state.

Math
NCTM Standards
- *Systematically collect, organize, and describe data*
- *Select and use an appropriate method for computing from among mental arithmetic, paper-and-pencil, calculator, and computer methods*
- *Make inferences and convincing arguments that are based on data analysis*

Estimation
Whole number operations
Formulas
Percent
Statistics
Graphs

Project 2061 Benchmarks
- *Locate information in reference books, back issues of newspapers and magazines, compact disks, and computer databases.*
- *Use numerical data in describing and comparing objects and events*

Social Science
Geography
Sociology

Processes
Predicting
Observing
Collecting and recording data
Comparing
Interpreting data
Inferring
Working cooperatively
Communicating ideas
Formulating questions
Considering multiple points of view
Appreciating rights/responsibilities

Materials
Resources: almanacs, atlases, encyclopedias, databases
Calculators
Colored pencils

Background Information
This activity is designed to be used as an introductory lesson in population or as an in-depth study in sociology. Choose the area of study which will best meet your needs.

To expose students to global population issues, compare continents or the top ten cities of the world. Do students know that the population of the world has passed five billion? How many more can the world handle, considering our resources? What about China's plan to limit each family to one child? Although the world's city boundaries are difficult to define and the various nations do not take a census at the same time, patterns and observations are still possible.

If the focus of your study is the United States, a comparison of growth in the nine regions of the country (as recorded in the almanac), individual states, or the top ten U.S. cities is recommended. One advantage of comparing states is that the almanacs generally list census data for every decade.

A study of state history might indicate research into the most populated cities within the state. Which ones are growing fastest? Check the local Chamber of Commerce for information on your own city.

Data can be supplied by the teacher or researched by the students. Almanacs and encyclopedias give the land area and the current population. To find past populations for cities, a 20-year old almanac may need to be found at the local library.

Use the following formulas to complete student activity sheets:

Density = Population/Area

% of Total population = Specific population/Total population
    Example: Louisiana population/Population of the U.S.

% Gain = [Present population - Past population]/Past population

% Loss = [Past population - Present population]/Past population

20-year projection =
    [Current population x Gain or Loss] + or - Current population

Births, deaths, and immigration are the three ways population changes. However, government policies (such as the People's Republic of China mandating only one child per family) and unexpectedly large groups of immigrants (such as those from Southeast Asia) can alter projected figures. A simple percent based on past history is a beginning way to predict the future population, but the field is really much more complex.

Management

1. Determine which type of locations the class will study (see *Background Information*).
2. If students are doing all the research themselves, allow about four class periods to complete the activity. Two periods are needed for research, one for calculations, and one for graphing and discussion.
3. Students should work in small groups.

Procedure

1. Ask the *Key Question*.
2. Student groups should research the past and present populations as well as land area of the chosen locations. You may prefer to supply part of the data. Area should be recorded according to the measurement standard used in the resources. Do not convert square miles into square kilometers.
3. Have students figure the percent of gain or loss and use it to make the 20-year projection.
4. Instruct students to compute the density of past, present, and future populations.
5. Students should find the percent of total population for past, present, and future populations. This column may not be applicable in some cases and can be left blank.
6. Have students answer the questions below the table.
7. Direct students to make a line graph showing the population trends, using a different color for each location.
8. Students should formulate their own questions and discuss the results.

Discussion

1. After completing your research, you have learned many things that have not been asked. From your results, what questions can be answered? What other questions would you like to ask? (The ideal situation would be for students to generate questions on their own.)
   Examples
   a. Has the number of people living in _____ increased or decreased over the stated years?
   b. Does growth over the past 20 years guarantee growth over the next 20 years? [No.] Why or why not? [Changes in number of births, deaths, and immigrants; physical space; jobs; etc.]
   c. How does population density affect living conditions?
   d. How does population affect representation in Congress? [Every state has two Senators but the number of Representatives are determined by population. After each census, adjustments are made whereby some states gain Representatives but others may lose them.]
   e. Which _____ show natural restraints affecting future growth?
   f. Which physical features may promote growth?
   g. Will growth reach the saturation point?
   h. Where are the heaviest concentrations of population?
   i. How will continued growth affect the world's natural resources?
   j. How can growth be slowed down or speeded up? How would your solutions affect people?

Extensions

1. Distribute an outline map and have students locate the places in their data table.
2. Students can draw a pictograph map indicating the density of each location. Make a key.

Curriculum Correlation

Language Arts

1. If given the opportunity, and considering your projected findings, in which metropolitan area would you choose to live and why?
2. Write letters to the Chamber of Commerce of each metropolitan area to compare population projections and to see what programs each city has to promote smooth growth increases.

Art

1. Draw an advertisement to lure people to your city, state, or continent.
2. Draw a cartoon of a saturated city.

People Plosion II

LOCATION	AREA: SQ.___	PAST - 20 YEARS AGO			PRESENT				FUTURE - 20 YEARS PROJ.		
		POPULATION	DENSITY	% OF TOTAL POP.	POPULATION	DENSITY	% OF TOTAL POP.	% + OR -	POPULATION	DENSITY	% OF TOTAL POP.

Which location shows the most projected growth? _____

_____ ...the least projected growth?

_____ ...the greatest density?

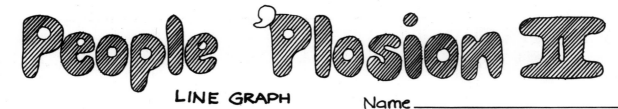

People 'Plosion II

LINE GRAPH

Name _____

Title _____

POPULATION IN (thousands, millions, billions)

1. Write the years below past, present, and future.

2. Plot the populations for each location and connect with a line. Use a different color for each location. Label the line.

PAST _____ PRESENT _____ FUTURE _____

Tic-Tac-Room

Topic
Coordinate grid

Key Question
How can we find places on a map?

Focus
Students will locate items in their classrooms using a life-size coordinate grid.

Math
NCTM Standards
- *Systematically collect, organize, and describe data*
- *Estimate, make, and use measurements to describe and compare phenomena*

Estimation
Measurement
   length
Coordinates

Project 2061 Benchmarks
- *Geometric figures, number sequences, graphs, diagrams, sketches, number lines, maps, and stories can be used to represent objects, events, and processes in the real world, although such representations can never be exact in every detail.*
- *Find and describe locations on maps with rectangular and polar coordinates.*

Social Science
Geography

Processes
Observing
Collecting and recording data
Comparing
Working cooperatively
Communicating ideas
Reading maps

Materials
Meter sticks
20-30 sheets of 8 1/2" x 11" paper
Masking tape
Optional: a string the room's length for each group

Background Information
Many maps use a grid system. The map index lists coordinates which make it easier to locate streets, cities, mountains, and other places.

A map grid differs from a graph of ordered pairs in at least two ways. First, the starting point (A-1) on a map is in the upper left corner. The letters and numbers may go in either direction. The starting point on a graph is either in the center if there are four quadrants or in the lower left corner if only the first quadrant (x and y both positive) is used. Second, it is the area between the lines that is important on a map. Geographic locations often cover an area larger than a point, a street for example. The identifying letters and numbers are written in the spaces between the lines. In contrast, a graph is numbered at the lines and there is a specific point that is plotted along the x and y axes.

Management
1. Groups of three or four are recommended.
2. If there are multiple objects of the same type, such as windows, specify which one is to be identified. Also discuss how to identify objects in more than one grid.
3. If students have difficulty estimating the grid coordinates, have them use string. One person should hold the string at the object while another stretches it perpendicular to one wall and parallel to the other. The coordinates can also be determined by having a person walk to the wall in line with the object.

Procedure
1. Ask the *Key Question*. Determine the starting corner. Two options are available depending on which direction is faced.
2. Have students measure and mark the meters along the length and width of the room. Put 20 cm strips of masking tape at each meter. Position them high enough so they are visible from any location in the room.
3. Students should make large (8 1/2" x 11") letter/number labels and mount them *between*, and at the same height as, the meter marks.
4. Instruct students to locate and label the coordinates of the teacher's desk as a class.
5. Agree upon and record classroom objects to be added to the list.
6. Have student groups record the coordinates of various objects in the room.
7. Discuss the results.

Discussion
1. What maps use this kind of coordinates? (Give students time to search for examples such as road maps, city, state, and national maps, etc.)

2. How are coordinates helpful? In what other ways could you be given directions to find a place on a map?

3. How are polar (latitude/longitude) coordinates different from the rectangular coordinates used in *Tic-Tac-Room*? [Polar coordinates refer to a specific point, while rectangular coordinates refer to a retangular area within a grid.]

4. What are the differences between a coordinate map grid and a coordinate graph? [See *Background Information*.]

Extensions

1. Use local city maps (check with the Chamber of Commerce), one per group for further coordinate practice. Give a location and ask for the coordinates or give the coordinates and ask for the street or object of your choice.

2. Take an existing map and make grids. Find various locations.

3. Play *Battleship*, the game or the computer simulation.

4. Give students directions such as "Jose, stand in B-7", "Where is the globe located?", or "Name an object in G-1."

Tic-Tac-Room

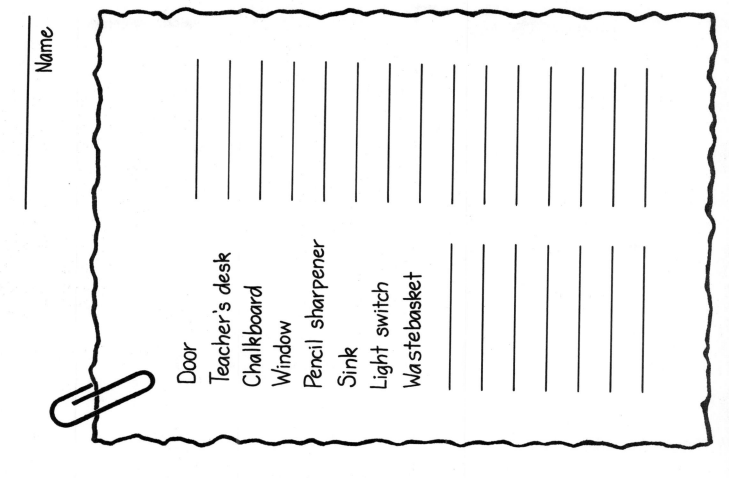

Name _____

Door

Teacher's desk

Chalkboard

Window

Pencil sharpener

Sink

Light switch

Wastebasket

Measure and label each meter along the length and width of your room. Label one side with letters and the other with numbers.

Identify the coordinates in which the objects in your classroom are located. Example:

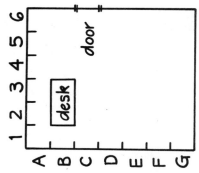

Door   C-6

Desk   B-2, B-3

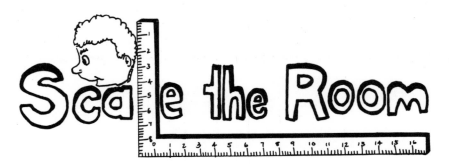

Topic
Scale drawing

Key Question
How can we fit this room onto a piece of paper?

Focus
The students will map their classroom or another room to scale.

Math
NCTM Standards
- *Understand and apply ratios, proportions, and percents in a wide variety of situations*
- *Estimate, make, and use measurements to describe and compare phenomena*

Estimation
  rounding
Measurement
  length
Whole number operations
Ratios

Project 2061 Benchmarks
- *Geometric figures, number sequences, graphs, diagrams, sketches, number lines, maps, and stories can be used to represent objects, events, and processes in the real world, although such representations can never be exact in every detail.*
- *Scale drawings show shapes and compare locations of things very different in size.*

Social Science
Geography

Processes
Observing
Collecting and recording data
Comparing
Interpreting data
Working cooperatively
Communicating ideas
Making maps

Materials
Meter sticks
Metric rulers
Calculators

Background Information
The scale format used by The National Geographic Society has been chosen for this book. Where a metric or standard length is used for actual and scale dimensions, a ratio is written first. Then a number comparison is written to the unit of measurement (example: 1:50 or 5 centimeters to the millimeter). When a non-standard measurement such as walking steps is converted to metrics, the ratio is omitted (example: 5 steps to the centimeter).

To figure the scale, develop a ratio between the room length and the graph paper squares. If the room length is 976 centimeters and you are using the 1/2 cm grid (46 squares long) in this activity, a good ratio might be 1:50 or 5 centimeters to the millimeter. This makes it easy to deal with remainders.

How was this figure determined? If 976 is divided by 46, the answer is 21.22. So the ratio must be at least 22 cm to a square. Since it is easier to count by 25's than by 22's and it is evenly divisible by 5 mm, 25 cm is a good choice. Another choice might be 30 cm.

Some of the items to consider for the classroom include bookcases, the teacher's desk, tables, student desks, the sink, a file cabinet, and closets. The placement of doors, windows, and chalkboards is also part of a complete map.

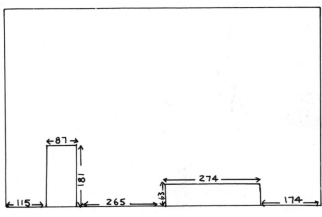

Rough scale drawing in centimeters.

Specific items are not difficult to measure, but what about their distance from each other or a door? It is helpful to make a simple sketch on scratch paper for recording measurements.

Management

1. Choose the room to be drawn to scale. The classroom has obvious advantages but, if the amount of furniture seems too much to handle, identify a few specific items with which students are to work.
2. Groups of three or four work well. Job titles might include recorder (records items and measurements), checker (keeps group on task, verifies accuracy), and workers (take measurements and do computation).
3. Consider giving each group a section of the room to map and combine these into one map or have each group map the entire room.
4. Since the scale will relate to centimeters, measure in centimeters rather than meters.
5. Square floor tiles can also be used as a measuring standard with each tile representing one graph paper square. Glue graph paper together, if needed, to get the dimensions of the room.

(Following is a different approach for presenting this lesson in addition to the usual *Procedure*. This is offered for those teachers whose students are prepared for more independent investigations.)

Open-ended: Ask the *Key Question* and challenge student groups to organize and produce the final product.

Procedure

1. Ask the Key *Question*. Review measuring and converting to scale with students.
2. Discuss which items should be represented on the map and have students record them in the first column of the activity sheet.

3. Student groups should measure and record the length and width of the items listed. Measurements may be recorded on the activity sheet or directly on a simple sketch of the room.
4. Agree upon a scale as a class or within individual groups.
5. Have students convert measurements to scale and record.
6. Student groups should construct a scale drawing of the room, starting with the perimeter.
7. Discuss and compare results.

Discussion

Before
1. What items should be included on our map?
2. What are some possible problems you might have gathering information? What are some solutions to these problems?

After
3. What professions use scale drawings? [cartographers, architects, contractors, landscapers, car designers, etc.]
4. Compare the problems a class might encounter with those of a builder or another professional.
5. How can knowing how to make a scale drawing be useful to you? [planning where to place furniture before moving into a place, etc.]

Extensions

1. Draw a room of your house to scale.
2. Select an object from a period of history being studied and draw it to scale. Examples: Mayflower, Statue of Liberty, Egyptian pyramid, Acropolis, etc.
3. Use the data from this activity for R*oom to Move*.

Scale the Room

Names _____

1. Measure and record the information needed.
2. Decide the scale: _____ to the _____
3. Compute the dimensions of each item to scale.
4. Draw the room to scale on the graph paper.

ITEM	LENGTH	WIDTH	SCALE LENGTH	SCALE WIDTH
Room				

_____

Scale _____ to 5 millimeters

_____ to the millimeter

_____

_____

Names

Room to Move

Topic
Room arrangement

Key Question
How will you arrange this room to best meet our needs?

Focus
Students will measure their classroom, take inventory of its furniture, and create an arrangement which maximizes floor space.

Math
NCTM Standards
- *Understand and apply ratios, proportions, and percents in a wide variety of situations*
- *Estimate, make, and use measurements to describe and compare phenomena*

Estimation
   rounding
Measurement
   length
Whole number operations
Ratios
Problem solving

Project 2061 Benchmarks
- *Geometric figures, number sequences, graphs, diagrams, sketches, number lines, maps, and stories can be used to represent objects, events, and processes in the real world, although such representations can never be exact in every detail.*
- *Scale drawings show shapes and compare locations of things very different in size.*

Social Science
Geography

Processes
Observing
Collecting and recording data
Comparing
Identifying and controlling variables
Interpreting data
Applying
Working cooperatively
Communicating ideas
Making maps
Considering multiple points of view

Materials
1/2 cm graph paper from *Scale the Room*
Meter sticks
Metric rulers
Scissors
Glue sticks
Calculators

Background Information
When planning where to place furniture, the purpose of the room and needs of the people using it must first be identified. Classroom considerations might include traffic patterns between desks, access to sink and storage areas, and special tools such as computers, trash cans, and files. Typical classroom desk rows, if used, should be at least 76 cm apart.

To figure scale, divide the length of the room by the number of squares along the length of the graph paper. For example, if the room is 976 cm long and the paper has 46 squares, the answer is 21.22. This means the ratio must be at least 22 cm to a square to fit on the paper. Since it is easier to count by 25's than 22"s and it is evenly divisible by 5 mm (the length of a square), 25 cm is a good choice. Another choice might be 30 cm.

The scale format used by The National Geographic Society has been chosen for this book. Where a metric or standard length is used for actual and scale dimensions, a ratio is written first. Then a number comparison is written to the unit of measurement (example: 1:50 or 5 centimeters to the millimeter). When a nonstandard measurement such as walking steps is converted to metrics, the ratio is omitted (example: 5 steps to the centimeter).

Management
1. Groups of four are suggested. Job descriptions might include pattern cutter, inventory manager, data recorder, and math technician.
2. Allow 50 minutes or more for initial discussion, inventory, and measuring.
3. The time needed to figure scale and prepare patterns will depend on student abilities and the patterns needed. Average-sized furniture patterns are included so students can focus on arrangement rather than scale drawing. Where furniture differs significantly, patterns will need to be prepared to scale. The patterns given are drawn to scale of 1:50 or 5 centimeters to the millimeter. If students have done *Scale the Room*, those pieces may be cut for use in this activity.
4. Room arranging and voting on the best arrangement will take another class period. Additional time should be allotted to move the furniture into the winning arrangement.

Procedure

1. Ask the *Key Question*, distribute the *Planning Sheet*, and guide a discussion of things to consider when arranging furniture.
2. Student groups should measure and record the length and width of the room in centimeters. Round all measurements to the nearest centimeter.
3. Have students take inventory and measure the furniture in the room.
4. Instruct students to find the scale dimensions, particularly of those items needed to supplement the patterns given.
5. Students should draw additional patterns and cut the number needed as recorded on the inventory.
6. Have students arrange the furniture patterns, considering the things discussed.
7. Students should glue the patterns on the graph paper after determing the best arrangement.
8. Have the groups present their arrangements to the class. Conduct a vote for the best arrangement.
9. *Optional:* Implement the winning arrangement so the class can evaluate the efficiency of the new design.

Discussion

1. What are the specialized needs of the room being arranged? [i.e., band room vs. art room – answers will vary]
2. What are the traffic patterns and how do they affect the arrangement of the classroom furniture?
3. How do the number of students in a class affect furniture arrangement? [If conditions are crowded, the furniture needs to be arranged more efficiently; some furniture may need to be removed.]
4. Why is there rarely one perfect room design? [Every classroom's needs are different.]
5. Will the winning design always be the best arrangement plan? [Not necessarily. Sometimes what looks good on paper is not practical in reality.]
6. When might you personally use the skill of drawing to scale? [deciding where furniture will go before moving into a place]

Extensions

1. Use the planning sheet to design another room at school (science lab, computer lab, home economics room) or home.
2. Invite an interior decorator to speak on room design and furniture arranging.

Curriculum Correlation

Language Arts

Write to the nearest college to find out what a person must study to become an interior designer.

Art

Design the ultimate classroom of the future, trying to anticipate needs and futuristic teaching aids.

Room to Move

PLANNING SHEET

Names _____
_____
_____
_____

Kind of Room: _____

	ACTUAL	SCALE
Length	_____	_____
Width	_____	_____
Area	_____	

Things to consider:

_____

_____

_____

SCALE _____ to the _____

_____

_____

_____

INVENTORY

Item	#	Actual Dimensions	Scale Dimensions	Item	#	Actual Dimensions	Scale Dimensions

Room to Move

These are some average furniture sizes. Yours may be different. Supplement with your own drawings and cut what is needed.

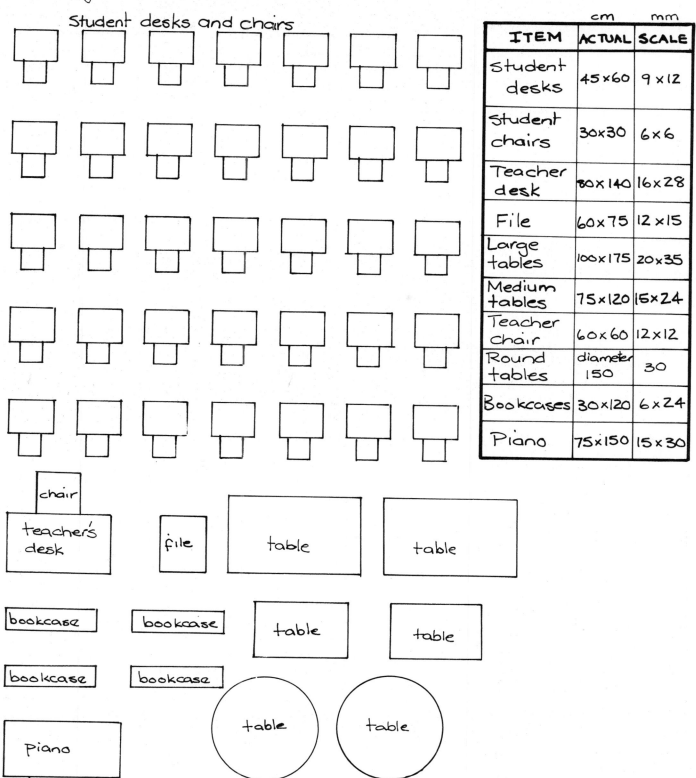

Student desks and chairs

ITEM	ACTUAL (cm)	SCALE (mm)
Student desks	45×60	9×12
Student chairs	30×30	6×6
Teacher desk	80×140	16×28
File	60×75	12×15
Large tables	100×175	20×35
Medium tables	75×120	15×24
Teacher chair	60×60	12×12
Round tables	diameter 150	30
Bookcases	30×120	6×24
Piano	75×150	15×30

chair

teacher's desk

file

table

table

bookcase

bookcase

table

table

bookcase

bookcase

table

table

Piano

113

SHRINKING BOUNDARIES

Topic
Scale drawing

Key Question
How do you shrink a basketball court?

Focus
Students will create a scale map of half of a basketball court. Maps will then be paired to complete a full court.

Math
NCTM Standards
- *Understand and apply ratios, proportions, and percents in a wide variety of situations*
- *Estimate, make, and use measurements to describe and compare phenomena*

Estimation
  rounding
Measurement
  length
Whole number operations
Ratios
Decimals

Project 2061 Benchmarks
- *Geometric figures, number sequences, graphs, diagrams, sketches, number lines, maps, and stories can be used to represent objects, events, and processes in the real world, although such representations can never be exact in every detail.*
- *Scale drawings show shapes and compare locations of things very different in size.*
- *The scale chosen for a graph or drawing makes a big difference in how useful it is.*

Social Science
Geography

Processes
Predicting
Observing
Collecting and recording data
Comparing
Interpreting data
Working cooperatively
Communicating ideas
Making maps

Materials
Meter sticks or tapes
Metric rulers
Graph paper, 1/4" or smaller
Drawing compasses

Background Information
A regulation basketball court is 94 by 50 feet or approximately 23 by 15 meters. Elementary school courts may vary due to space or other factors.

To determine the scale, develop a ratio between the longest measurement and the graph paper squares. If the longest measurement is 12 meters and the length of the paper is 43 squares, the scale of 1 meter = 3 squares would be a good choice.

Management
1. This activity may take one or two 60-minute periods, depending on student abilities.
2. Groups of four are recommended. An even number of groups are needed for pairing maps.
3. Decide on the standard for rounding. The nearest meter may be easy, but not very accurate for shorter measurements. The nearest decimeter is a good choice.
4. Students should record actual lengths in decimals. For example, a measurement of 13 meters 78 centimeters should be recorded as 13.78 meters. Rounded to the nearest decimeter, it would be 13.8 meters.
5. Although graph paper is suggested, capable students may wish to do the scale drawing on blank paper. The scale would be meters to centimeters or millimeters.
6. Accuracy will be determined by pairing group maps at the end of the activity.

(Following are two different approaches for presenting this lesson in addition to the usual *Procedure*. These are offered for those teachers whose students are prepared for more independent investigations.)

Open-ended: Ask the *Key Question* and have student groups devise their own plan for recreating the basketball court on a paper of specified size.
Guided Planning: Present the following questions, one at a time, to help student groups organize their investigation of the *Key Question.*
1. What measurements need to be taken?
2. How are you going to organize the recording of measurements?
3. What supplies do you need?
4. List the responsibilities of each group member.
5. What scale will you need to fit the drawing on the paper?

Procedure
1. Ask the *Key Question*. Distribute the activity sheet and review the parts of a basketball court. Discuss measuring and drawing to scale.

2. Have student groups go to the court and estimate the total length and width.
3. Students should measure and record the actual and rounded lengths in the table.
4. Direct students to calculate the scale needed to re-create the basketball court on the paper you have chosen. Give guidance as needed.
5. Have students figure the scale measure or number in the last column. To pair maps, all groups must use the same scale.
6. Students should complete the scale drawings. A compass is useful for drawing the circles. The mid-point of each line must be found first.
7. Have each group pair their map with another group's map to make a full court.

Discussion
1. What is the value of drawing to scale?
2. What professions use scale drawings? [cartographers, architects, pool designers, interior decorators, furniture designers, landscapers, etc.]
3. Was this court ever drawn to scale? [probably before it was placed on the playground]

Extensions
1. Take another playground court or area and draw it to scale.
2. Locate maps which use scale. Complete a table with the name of the book, kind of map, and scale ratio.

SHRINKING BOUNDARIES

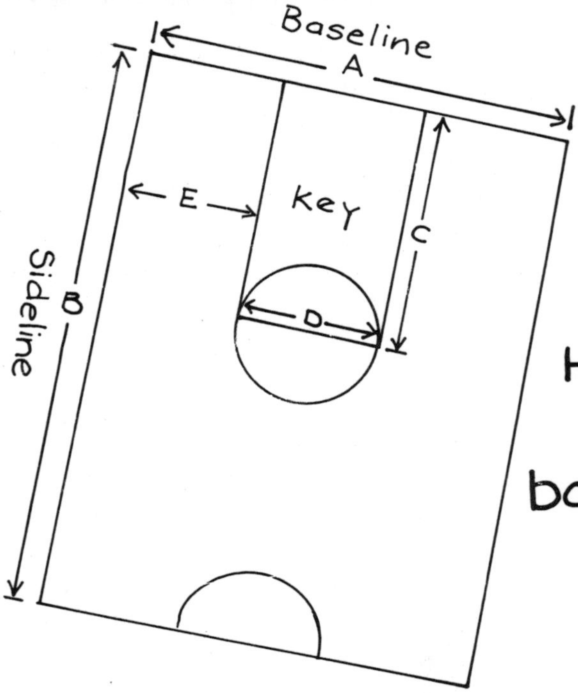

Baseline

A

Key

E

C

D

Sideline

B

I

_____

_____

_____

Cartographers

How do you shrink a basketball court?

FULL COURT	
LENGTH	WIDTH

PREDICT _____ _____

ACTUAL _____ _____

SCALE _____ to the _____

	LINE	LENGTH		
		ACTUAL	ROUNDED	SCALE
A	Baseline			
	Baseline/2			
B	Sideline			
C	Baseline to free throw line			
D	Free throw line			
	Free throw line/2			
E	Sideline to key			

Bird's eye view

Topic
School design

Key Question
If you could plan a new school, how would it look?

Focus
Students will create a school site which will meet specific needs.

Math
NCTM Standards
- *Visualize and represent geometric figures with special attention to developing spatial sense*
- *Develop an appreciation of geometry as a means of describing the physical world*

Geometry and spatial sense

Project 2061 Benchmarks
- *Geometric figures, number sequences, graphs, diagrams, sketches, number lines, maps, and stories can be used to represent objects, events, and processes in the real world, although such representations can never be exact in every detail.*

Social Science
Geography

Processes
Observing
Collecting and recording data
Comparing
Identifying and controlling variables
Applying
Working cooperatively
Communicating ideas
Making maps
Considering multiple points of view

Materials
Large white or manila construction paper
Crayons or colored pencils
Metric rulers

Background Information
An architect can draw a school in many ways. Traditional schools have long classroom wings, but new designs have been tried in recent years. These include open-space rooms and nearly square buildings with classroom clusters. The factors an architect must consider are discussed in the fact sheet, *School Architecture.*

Management
1. This project can be used to redesign the school the students attend or to create a school for a different setting and needs. It will take several class periods.
2. Students may create individual designs or work in pairs.
3. The chart with brainstorming ideas should be in sight during the entire project.
3. Emphasize that the design should be a floor plan, not a side-view drawing.
4. If some actual blueprints are brought for the class to examine, students will notice symbols for such things as windows, doors, cabinets, and plumbing. Decide which details are important for your purpose and which can be eliminated.

Procedure
Introductory Activities
1. Begin with a tour of the school plant.
2. In small groups, have students brainstorm the things to be considered when designing a school. Write group ideas on a chart or butcher paper as they are shared with the total class.
3. Have students study the brainstorming chart and *School Architecture*, decide which factors are most important, and complete the top part of the planning sheet.

Designing Time
4. Agree on symbols for door, windows, etc. If possible, study an actual floor plan with the class.
5. Students should work on their school designs.

Concluding Activities
6. Have students write a paragraph describing for whom their school was made and attach it to their designs.
7. Display finished designs or allow time for oral presentations.

Discussion
1. How does your school fit the needs for which it was designed?
2. Does this school use space economically or did that matter?
3. What costs must be considered when building a school? [land, construction material, crew, finish work like painting, landscaping, etc.]
4. How expensive do you think your school would be to build?
5. When was our school built? How expensive do you think it was to build this school? (Check with the

district business manager to obtain the data for your school and other schools in your district.)

Extension
Compare school styles in your town. Are pictures available?

Curriculum Correlation
Math
1. Make a bar graph comparing the building costs of different schools in your district. Include the years they were built.

2. Using a scale ratio, find the approximate floor area to determine how much color tile or carpeting will be needed. Obtain the current price from a local store and compute the cost.

Art
   Draw a side-view of the school complete with school name.

Literature
   Read *How a House Happens* by Jan Adkins (1983).

Bird's eye view

What must you consider when designing a school?

FACTOR	OUR SCHOOL
number of students	_____
_____	_____
_____	_____
_____	_____
_____	_____
_____	_____
_____	_____
_____	_____
_____	_____

Complete the following paragraph and attach it to your architectural plan.

This school was designed for _____

_____

_____

_____

_____

_____

_____

School Architecture

Factors to Consider

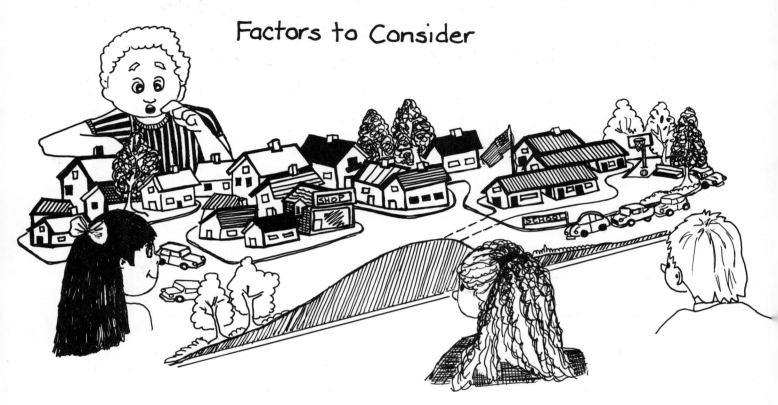

1. **NEIGHBORHOOD**

   a. **Urban**: high population density, industries and business, culturally rich environment, many apartment dwellers, multicultural, scarce land <u>Conclusion</u>- The school needs to conserve space.

   b. **Suburban**: mostly single family homes, little business or industry, commuter population, less ethnic diversity, highly mobile residents

   c. **Rural**: farming or ranching families, permanent and seasonal workers, single family homes, spread out <u>Conclusion</u> -One school serves a large area.

2. **ARCHITECTURE**

   What is the style of the buildings in the surrounding area?

3. PHYSICAL CHARACTERISTICS

a. Room size - What is the proposed class size?
b. Purpose of the room - multi (auditorium, cafeteria) or single use
c. Placement of windows, number and position of electrical outlets
d. Sound - Is there an airport, train station, or large business nearby?
e. Climate

4. LANDSCAPE

What will be planted on the grounds? Where?

5. PLAYGROUND

What play areas and equipment are needed? Where?

6. SAFETY

a. Access for the handicapped
b. Location of streets, roads and highways
c. Businesses and / or buildings nearby

7. STUDENT BODY

a. Students with special needs such as the handicapped
b. Special grading system (K-2, 3-6, K-8, etc.)
c. All-boy or all-girl

8. SPECIAL SERVICES

What kind of space is needed for counselors, the nurse, the secretary, administrators, the music teacher, the p.e. teacher, and others?

The final consideration concerns not only the architect but also those who attend. A school is a place for students to formulate ideas and use the information given. A school should be a place which is functional and pleasing to attend.

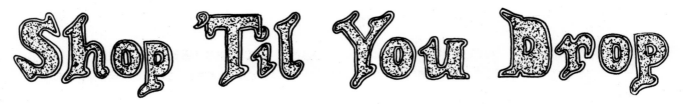
Shop 'Til You Drop

Topic
Scale model

Key Question
How will your mall compare with others in your class?

Focus
Students will create a floor plan of a shopping mall and convert it into a three-dimensional model.

Math
NCTM Standards
- *Visualize and represent geometric figures with special attention to developing spatial sense*
- *Develop an appreciation of geometry as a means of describing the physical world*
- *Select appropriate units and tools to measure to the degree of accuracy required in a particular situation*

Measurement
  length
Whole number operations
Ratios
Geometry and spatial sense

Project 2061 Benchmark
- *Geometric figures, number sequences, graphs, diagrams, sketches, number lines, maps, and stories can be used to represent objects, events, and processes in the real world, although such representations can never be exact in every detail.*

Social Science
Geography

Processes
Observing
Collecting and recording data
Comparing
Interpreting data
Applying
Working cooperatively
Communicating ideas
Making and reading maps
Considering multiple points of view

Materials
Colored construction paper
Cardboard or plywood base for each model
Metric rulers
Graph paper
Crayons or colored pencils
Tape and glue

Background Information
Architects often make scale models when presenting their projects to potential buyers. Sometimes models are used during a court trial. When transforming a map to a model, scale becomes a subject of concern. If students are given opportunities to experience the physical transfer, the process becomes more personalized.

The scale format used by The National Geographic Society includes a ratio followed by the relationship to a unit of measure (example: 1:50 or 5 centimeters to the millimeter).

Management
1. Groups of two to four are suggested.
2. This activity will take several class periods.
3. When the class is ready to construct their models, show them how to make rectangular buildings from construction paper. Ignore the tabs if tape is used instead of glue.

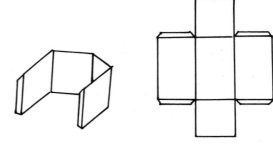

4. Model size will be determined by space and available base materials.
5. Other settings to consider for the scale model might include a town, harbor, farm, magazine scene, etc.

Procedure
1. Have students brainstorm types and sizes of buildings they may find in a mall.
2. Ask the *Key Question* and instruct student groups to design a mall (or another setting you have chosen) on graph or plain paper. It is helpful to start with a rough sketch.
3. Students should measure each store or structure on the drawing and record the dimensions on the activity sheet.
4. Have students measure their cardboard or plywood base and decide on a scale ratio. They should record and draw a line scale on the activity sheet.

5. Direct students to convert the map dimensions to model dimensions and record.
6. Students should build the model using construction paper and other materials.
7. Have students give an oral presentation about their design.

Discussion

1. How do the malls differ from each other? How are they the same? How do they compare to those in your area?
2. How did you decide what stores to put in your mall? [ideas from malls you have visited, stores that appeal to you, etc.]
3. Is your mall specialized? [built for the community, a certain age group, etc.]

4. How difficult was it to make a three-dimensional model from a two-dimensional drawing?

Extensions

1. Create a "rug town" or "rug farm" for a kindergarten class. Using pieces of fabric, enlarge a two-dimensional version of the plan on rug scraps sewn together. This creates a play area for use with toy cars, boats, or animals.
2. Use a grid system for reproducing a picture. Draw grid lines on the picture. Then reproduce the image within each square onto a larger piece of paper.

Curriculum Correlation

Art
   Landscape the model.

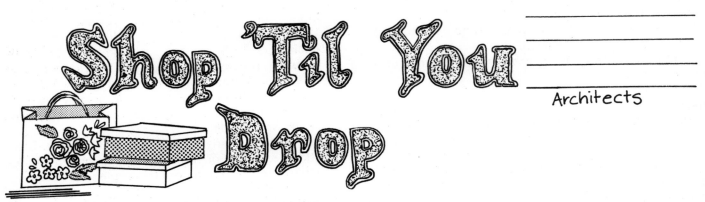

Shop 'Til You Drop

_____
_____
_____
Architects

We have chosen to design and build a_____.

Scale ___:___ or _____ to the _____

0 |————.............

STORE/STRUCTURE	DRAWING DIMENSIONS	SCALE MODEL DIMENSIONS

Continue the table on the back if needed.

Navigating Numerically

Topic
U.S. road numbering patterns

Key Question
You parachute from an airplane somewhere in the United States. You scramble out from under your silken canopy. The first thing you see is an interstate road sign. Where in the United States are you?

Focus
Students will discover the system used for numbering interstate highways.

Math
NCTM Standards
- *Verify and interpret results with respect to the original problem situation*
- *Recognize and apply deductive and inductive reasoning*
- *Describe, extend, analyze, and create a wide variety of patterns*

Patterns
Problem solving
Logic

Project 2061 Benchmarks
- *Mathematics is the study of many kinds of patterns, including numbers and shapes and operations on them. Sometimes patterns are studied because they help to explain how the world works or how to solve practical problems, sometimes because they are interesting in themselves.*
- *Sometimes people invent a general rule to explain how something works by summarizing observations. But people tend to overgeneralize, imagining general rules on the basis of only a few observations.*

Social Science
Geography
  United States

Processes
Observing
Collecting and recording data
Comparing
Interpreting data
Inferring
Generalizing

Applying
Working cooperatively
Communicating ideas
Reading maps

Materials
For each group
  U.S. road map

Background Information
There are three major types of roadways criss-crossing the United States.

 Interstate highways cross through more than one state.

 U.S. highways (federal) often connect interstates and can pass through more than one state.

 State highways are maintained inside state borders. If the road continues into another state, it receives another designation.

Interstates with three numbers (I-495) are radial, loop, or spur alternate routes. The last two digits (I-95) represent the number of the main route. These three-digit interstates often skirt around or encircle large metropolitan areas.

Business loops or spurs are one- or two-digit numbers on green signs. These indicate a convenient route through the business section of a city.

Some north/south roads may, for short distances, veer off in an east/west direction. The same is true of some east/west roads, which may veer off in a north/south direction. See *Interstate Highways* and *U.S. Highways* for further information.

Management
1. Students may work in groups of three to five, depending on available maps.
2. This activity can be done in one class period.
3. Do not show students the fact sheets until after they have explored the maps and discovered the interstate numbering pattern.

(Following is a different approach for presenting this lesson in addition to the usual *Procedure*. This is offered for those teachers whose students are pre-pared for more independent investigations.)

Open-ended: Ask the *Key Question* and have student groups plan how they will explore interstate numbering patterns and report their findings.

Procedure
1. Read aloud the *Key Question* with the parachute scenario. Discuss the information an interstate road sign would give.
2. Distribute the first activity sheet. Reread the scenario together and state the problem.
3. Give each student group a road map, the *Post Office State Abbreviations,* and the activity map.
4. Have students study the road map and fill in the table. To make the patterns more recognizable, students should draw the interstate highway locations on the activity map.
5. Students should describe the patterns they have discovered.
6. Lead a class discussion.

Discussion
1. Can you tell exactly where you are by looking at an interstate sign? [No.]
2. Can you tell *approximately* where you are? [Yes, if you know the pattern. You are in the eastern fourth of the country around the states of Georgia, Tennessee, Kentucky, and Ohio.]
3. What information does an interstate road sign give you? [just a number]
4. What other kinds of signs, along with the interstate sign, might help you know exactly where you are? [a junction sign with another highway, road mileage signs to various cities, etc.]
5. What else, beside signs, could give you clues to your location? [vegetation, climate]
6. What kind of numbers run east/west? [even] ...north/south? [odd]
7. Where are smaller numbers found? [in the South and West] ...larger numbers? [in the North and East]
8. Find some three-digit roads on the map. Where do you usually find signs with three digits? [around large metropolitan areas] What do you think three-digits indicate? [an interstate that bypasses a city or is an alternate route]
9. What other types of roads are shown on your road map? What symbols are used?

Extensions
1. Discover the pattern for numbering U.S. or Federal highways. (See *U.S. Highways.*)
2. Study other symbols shown in the road map key.
3. Make a large class map showing major interstates.

Curriculum Correlation
Math
1. Using the scale, determine the approximate length of major interstates in kilometers or miles. Make a comparison graph.
2. Determine the time needed to travel the full length of the U.S. following a 55 mph speed limit.

Language Arts
   Discuss the variety of terms used to name roads: highway, interstate, freeway, parkway, turnpike, toll road.

Economics
   Have students search some ways money is raised for road repair and upkeep. [Taxes, tolls, trucker's fees, etc.]

Navigating Numerically

You parachute from an airplane somewhere in the United States. You scramble out from under your silken canopy. The first thing you see is an interstate road sign.

Where in the United States are you?

Don't panic! You are not lost! There is a way to tell approximately where you are. On your U.S. map, locate the interstates listed below. Complete the table and map drawing to discover the interstate numbering system.

INTERSTATE	DIRECTION	STATES ALONG ROUTE
I-5	N-S	CA, OR, WA
I-70		
I-40		
I-25		
I-15		
I-10		
I-77		
I-94		
I-55		
I-95		

Describe the numbering system patterns you have found.

_____

_____

_____

Navigating Numerically

CT MI MN MS MO MT NE NV NH NJ NM NY NC ND OH

ID IL IN IA KS KY LA ME MD MA

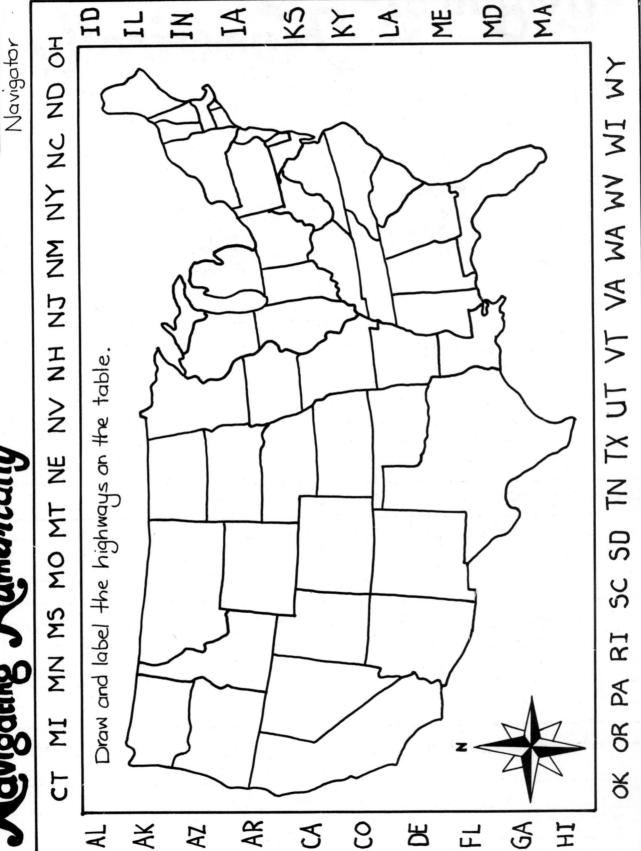

Draw and label the highways on the table.

AL AK AZ AR CA CO DE FL GA HI

OK OR PA RI SC SD TN TX UT VT VA WA WV WI WY

N

128

Navigating Numerically

OFFICIAL POST OFFICE STATE ABBREVIATIONS

AL	Alabama		MT	Montana
AK	Alaska		NE	Nebraska
AZ	Arizona		NV	Nevada
AR	Arkansas		NH	New Hampshire
CA	California		NJ	New Jersey
CO	Colorado		NM	New Mexico
CT	Connecticut		NY	New York
DE	Delaware		NC	North Carolina
FL	Florida		ND	North Dakota
GA	Georgia		OH	Ohio
HI	Hawaii		OK	Oklahoma
ID	Idaho		OR	Oregon
IL	Illinois		PA	Pennsylvania
IN	Indiana		RI	Rhode Island
IA	Iowa		SC	South Carolina
KS	Kansas		SD	South Dakota
KY	Kentucky		TN	Tennessee
LA	Louisiana		TX	Texas
ME	Maine		UT	Utah
MD	Maryland		VT	Vermont
MA	Massachusetts		VA	Virginia
MI	Michigan		WA	Washington
MN	Minnesota		WV	West Virginia
MS	Mississippi		WI	Wisconsin
MO	Missouri		WY	Wyoming

Navigating Numerically

INTERSTATE HIGHWAYS

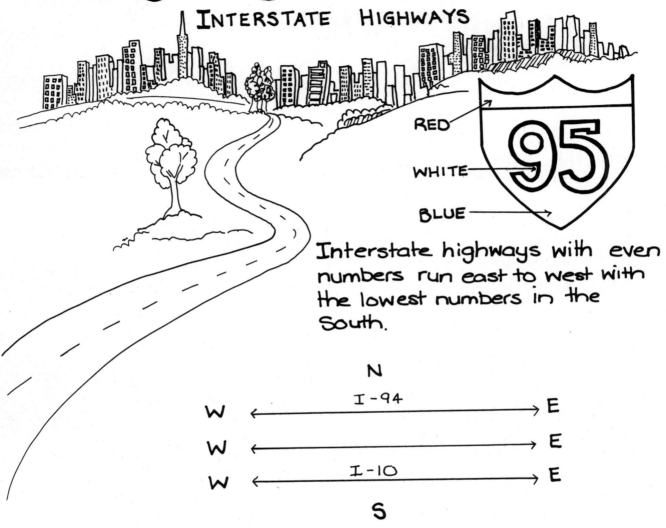

RED

WHITE

BLUE

Interstate highways with even numbers run east to west with the lowest numbers in the South.

Interstate highways with odd numbers run north and south with the lowest numbers in the West.

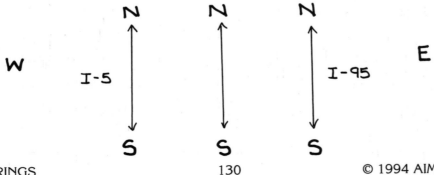

Navigating Numerically

U.S. Highways

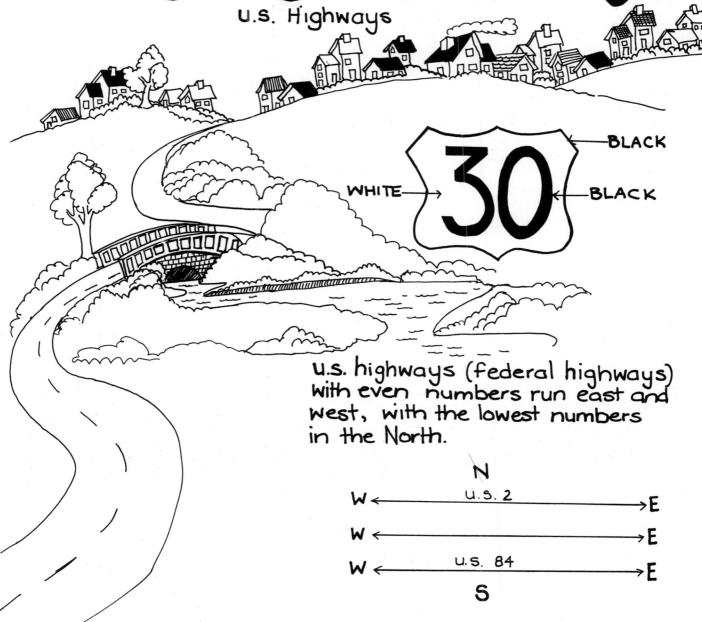

BLACK

WHITE → 30 ← BLACK

U.s. highways (federal highways) with even numbers run east and west, with the lowest numbers in the North.

N

W ←——— u.s. 2 ———→ E

W ←——————————→ E

W ←——— u.s. 84 ———→ E

S

U.s. highways (federal highways) with odd numbers run north and south, with the lowest numbers in the East.

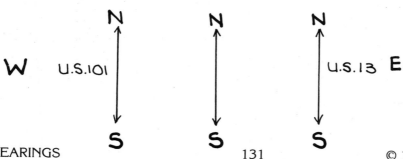

N   N   N

W   U.S.101   U.S.13 E

S   S   S

Rallying Around

Topic
U.S. road map

Key Question
You have been chosen to participate in a "See America Road Rally." You will be allowed to pick five cities at random to visit. After choosing your five cities, how long do you think your trip will take?

Focus
Students will use a U.S. road map to measure and compare distances between certain randomly selected cities while participating in a road rally simulation.

Math
NCTM Standards
- *Estimate, make, and use measurements to describe and compare phenomena*
- *Compute with whole numbers, fractions, decimals, integers, and rational numbers*

Estimation
   rounding
Measurement
   length
Whole number operations
Formulas
Ratios
Decimals

Project 2061 Benchmarks
- *In making decisions, it helps to take time to consider the benefits and drawbacks of alternatives.*
- *Measurements are always likely to give slightly different numbers, even if what is being measured stays the same.*
- *Estimate distances and travel times from maps and the actual size of objects from scale drawings.*

Social Science
Geography
   United States

Processes
Predicting
Observing
Collecting and recording data
Comparing
Interpreting data
Applying
Working cooperatively
Communicating ideas
Reading maps

Materials
For each group
   2 meters of kite string
   crayons or markers
   rulers
   calculators
   U.S. road map

Background Information
While this activity is structured to resemble a road rally to spark student interest, the major objectives include reading a road map, identifying the most direct route between two places, and using a scale of miles. Students are also asked to locate and label selected cities and to identify states.

During the rally, students must use a constant average speed of 55 mph, but reality dictates that road conditions, traffic, weather, and other factors might affect travel speed. The speed variable is controlled to ensure fair comparisons between groups. Miles, rather than kilometers, are used because mileage information is more commonly available. Most road maps have kilometer scales which can be used, if you wish, along with a metric speed limit. The *Driving Distance Chart* would not be applicable.

The easiest way to convert the map's scale distance to actual distance is to figure out the number of miles per centimeter. If an accurate estimate is made, this figure can be multiplied by the measured string length to obtain the actual distance. An alternative would be to construct a longer version of the map's scale distance and lay the string along it.

Management
1. Students should work in groups of four or five. The activity will take about 60 minutes.
2. Decide the number of hours which may be driven each day. Five or ten hours would facilitate the mathematics for lower grade students. Numbers such as six or eight hours would make the mathematics more challenging.
3. To prepare the string, put tape around one end to mark the beginning of the group's measurements. As students reach each city, they will make a mark on the string. Their string measurements will be approximate.

Procedure
1. Ask the *Key Question* and distribute the map/city card sheet. Have student groups cut out the city cards, lay them face down, and mix them up. Five cards should be drawn, indicating the cities on their road rally route.

2. Instruct students to locate the cities on a U.S. road map and record them on the blank map.
3. Give groups the second activity sheet and have them list their five cities, along with their states, in column one of the table.
4. Have students complete the second column, matching the numbers in column one. Note that the second column is numbered differently.
5. Decide the number of driving hours allowed per day and direct students to calculate the maximum number of miles allowed per day. Students must stop driving for the day when they reach one of their five cities even if they haven't driven the limit.
6. Reread the *Key Question* and have students make a prediction about the length of their trip.
7. Using the map scale, students should carefully estimate and record the number of miles equivalent to one centimeter.
8. Instruct students to place the string along the contours of each road and measure the distance between each city to the nearest tenth of a centimeter. Record as a decimal. Students must return to their city of origin to complete the rally.
9. Have students figure the actual travel distance. One method is to multiply the marked string length times the number of miles in one centimeter.
10. On the blank map, students should draw straight lines between the cities to show their route and write the actual distances on the lines.

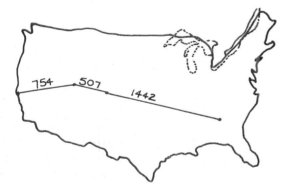

11. Have students use the time formula on the activity sheet to figure hours. Decimals should be rounded to the nearest tenth.
12. Direct students to calculate the number of days used according to the rules.
13. Students should compute all totals. If there is a tie between two or more groups for the least number of days, look at the hour totals.
14. Have students compare their distances and times with the *Driving Distance Chart*.
15. Discuss as a class.

Discussion
1. How long did your rally take?
2. What was the shortest leg of your trip? ...the longest leg?

3. How did you decide the order in which to visit your five cities?
4. What kinds of problems did you have deciding the most direct route? How did you resolve these problems?
5. Through how many states did your rally take you? What were they?
6. What different regions did you visit?
7. Compare distance estimates with groups who traveled to some of the same cities.

Extensions
1. Redo the activity using "as the crow flies" distances.
2. Obtain an airline schedule. Compare driving time to flight time. Should you include the wait at the airport?
3. Determine which two cities are farthest apart.
4. Pin one road map to a bulletin board. Using different color yarn, trace each group's trip. Pin paper markers showing the order. Paper cars can be placed at the city of origin.
5. Make a graph which compares the groups' distances and times.
6. Discuss how time zones affect traveling.

Curriculum Correlation
Language Arts
1. Write out directions for someone who would like to follow your route.
2. Research cities visited to learn about founding date, points of interest, etc. Design a travel brochure.

Art
1. Draw road signs that might have been seen along the way.
2. Design a poster advertising the "See America Road Rally."

Technology
   Use the "Travel Agent" option in the computer program, *Survival Math*, from Sunburst Communications, Inc.

Games
1. "Scotland Yard" from Milton Bradley
2. "Vacation" from Rand McNally

Home Link
   Encourage students to be a road map navigator on the next family trip.

Rallying Around

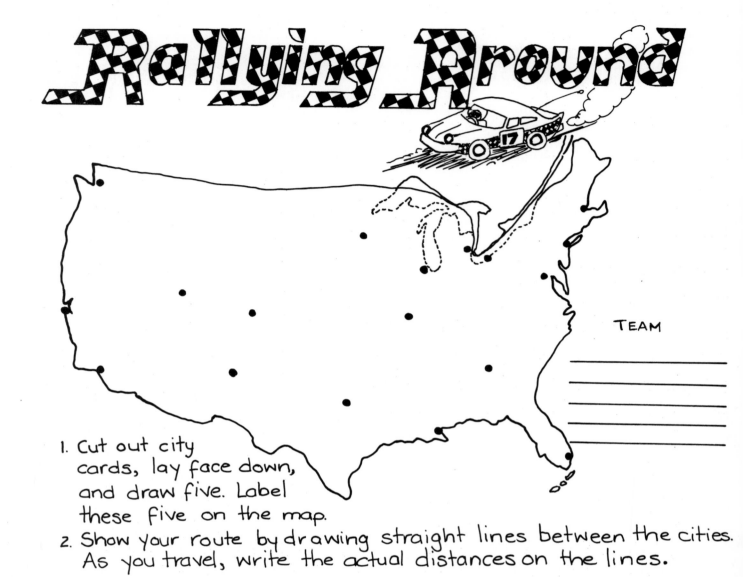

TEAM

_____
_____
_____
_____
_____

1. Cut out city cards, lay face down, and draw five. Label these five on the map.
2. Show your route by drawing straight lines between the cities. As you travel, write the actual distances on the lines.

Albuquerque	Denver	New York City
Atlanta	Detroit	St. Louis
Boston	Los Angeles	Salt Lake City
Chicago	Miami	San Francisco
Cleveland	Minneapolis	Seattle
Dallas	New Orleans	Washington, D. C.

Rallying Around

1. In the first column, list the five cities on your itinerary. The first should be closest to your hometown. List other cities in the most logical order. Remember, you must return to the first city.

2. Complete the second column, matching the numbers in the first column.

3. You may drive ____ hours per day. The speed limit is 55 mph. The maximum number of miles per day will be ____. You must stop driving for the day if you reach a city.

How many days do you think your road rally will take? [ ]

4. You are now ready to start your "See America Road Rally." Use string and scale of miles to measure distances. Travel the most direct route.

MAP SCALE: _____ miles to the centimeter

CITIES, STATES		ROADS TRAVELED	DISTANCE		TIME	
FROM	TO		STRING	ACTUAL	HOURS (to 10th)	DAYS
1.	2.					
2.	3.					
3.	4.					
4.	5.					
5.	1.					
				TOTAL		

Time = $\dfrac{\text{Distance}}{\text{Rate}}$

How many days did your road rally actually take? [ ]

Rallying Around

Driving Distance Chart

Legend

518	= Distance in miles
10:14	= Driving Time

These distances and driving times represent the most favorable commonly traveled routes under normal conditions.

Driving Times are average times within posted speed limits, excluding stops.

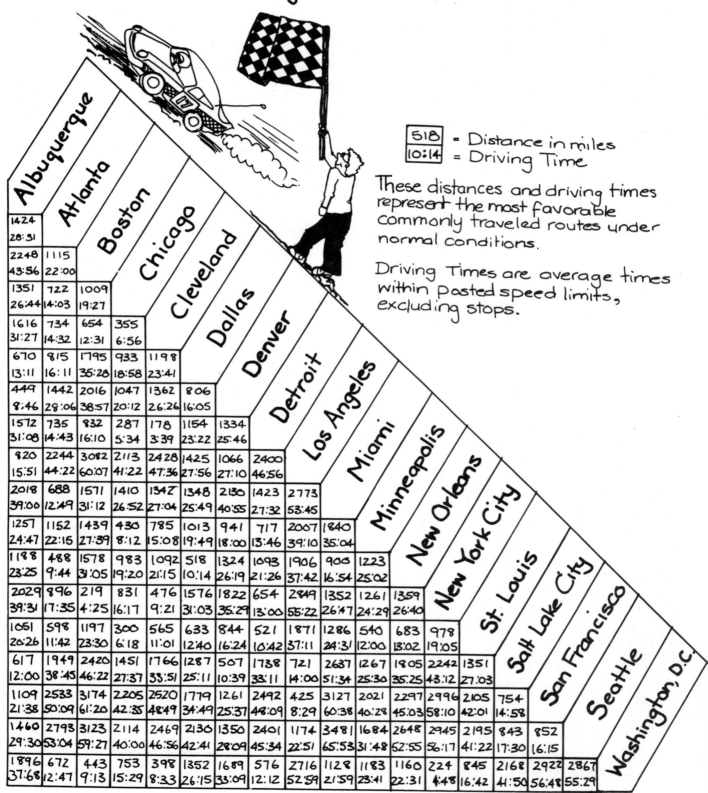

Each cell shows *distance in miles* over *driving time (hours:minutes)*.

To ↓ \ From →	Albuquerque	Atlanta	Boston	Chicago	Cleveland	Dallas	Denver	Detroit	Los Angeles	Miami	Minneapolis	New Orleans	New York City	St. Louis	Salt Lake City	San Francisco	Seattle
Atlanta	1424 / 28:31																
Boston	2248 / 43:56	1115 / 22:00															
Chicago	1351 / 26:44	722 / 14:03	1009 / 19:27														
Cleveland	1616 / 31:27	734 / 14:32	654 / 12:31	355 / 6:56													
Dallas	670 / 13:11	815 / 16:11	1795 / 35:28	933 / 18:58	1198 / 23:41												
Denver	449 / 8:46	1442 / 28:06	2016 / 38:57	1047 / 20:12	1362 / 26:26	806 / 16:05											
Detroit	1572 / 31:08	735 / 14:43	832 / 16:10	287 / 5:34	178 / 3:39	1154 / 23:22	1334 / 25:46										
Los Angeles	820 / 15:51	2244 / 44:22	3082 / 60:07	2113 / 41:22	2428 / 47:36	1425 / 27:56	1066 / 27:10	2400 / 46:56									
Miami	2018 / 39:00	688 / 12:49	1571 / 31:12	1410 / 26:52	1342 / 27:04	1348 / 25:49	2130 / 40:55	1423 / 27:32	2773 / 53:45								
Minneapolis	1257 / 24:47	1152 / 22:15	1439 / 27:39	430 / 8:12	785 / 15:08	1013 / 19:49	941 / 18:00	717 / 13:46	2007 / 39:10	1840 / 35:04							
New Orleans	1188 / 23:25	488 / 9:44	1578 / 31:05	983 / 19:20	1092 / 21:15	518 / 10:14	1324 / 26:19	1093 / 21:26	1906 / 37:42	900 / 16:54	1223 / 25:02						
New York City	2029 / 39:31	896 / 17:35	219 / 4:25	831 / 16:17	476 / 9:21	1576 / 31:03	1822 / 35:29	654 / 13:00	2849 / 55:22	1352 / 26:47	1261 / 24:29	1359 / 26:40					
St. Louis	1051 / 20:26	598 / 11:42	1197 / 23:30	300 / 6:18	565 / 11:01	633 / 12:40	844 / 16:24	521 / 10:42	1871 / 37:11	1286 / 24:31	540 / 12:00	683 / 13:02	978 / 19:05				
Salt Lake City	617 / 12:00	1949 / 38:45	2420 / 46:22	1451 / 27:37	1766 / 33:51	1287 / 25:11	507 / 10:39	1738 / 33:11	721 / 14:00	2637 / 51:34	1267 / 25:30	1805 / 35:25	2242 / 43:12	1351 / 27:03			
San Francisco	1109 / 21:38	2533 / 50:09	3174 / 61:20	2205 / 42:35	2520 / 48:49	1779 / 34:49	1261 / 25:37	2492 / 48:09	425 / 8:29	3127 / 60:38	2021 / 40:28	2297 / 45:03	2996 / 58:10	2105 / 42:01	754 / 14:58		
Seattle	1460 / 29:30	2793 / 53:04	3123 / 59:27	2114 / 40:00	2469 / 46:56	2130 / 42:41	1350 / 28:09	2401 / 45:34	1174 / 22:51	3481 / 65:53	1684 / 31:48	2648 / 52:55	2945 / 56:17	2195 / 41:22	843 / 17:30	852 / 16:15	
Washington, D.C.	1896 / 37:68	672 / 12:47	443 / 9:13	753 / 15:29	398 / 8:33	1352 / 26:15	1689 / 33:09	576 / 12:12	2716 / 52:59	1128 / 21:59	1183 / 23:41	1160 / 22:31	224 / 4:48	845 / 16:42	2168 / 41:50	2922 / 56:48	2867 / 55:29

What a Relief!

Topic
Relief maps

Key Question
How can you turn flour, salt, and water into a map?

Focus
Students will construct a flour-salt relief map of an area of study such as a state, country, or continent.

Math
NCTM Standard
- *Make and use measurements in problems and everyday situations*

Measurement
  volume

Project 2061 Benchmarks
- *Measure and mix dry and liquid materials (in the kitchen, garage, or laboratory) in prescribed amounts, exercising reasonable safety.*
- *Geometric figures, number sequences, graphs, diagrams, sketches, number lines, maps, and stories can be used to represent objects, events, and processes in the real world, although such representations can never be exact in every detail.*

Social Science
Geography
  topography

Processes
Observing
Comparing
Interpreting data
Applying
Working cooperatively
Communicating ideas
Making maps

Materials
For each map:
  250 ml (1 c.) flour
  125 ml (1/2 c.) salt
  125 ml (1/2 c.) water
  cardboard base and outline map, same size
  toothpicks
  gummed labels or masking tape
  tongue depressor, *optional*

For each table:
  bowls or trimmed milk containers
  glue and tape
  measuring cups and spoons
  butcher paper

For the class:
  sample relief map
  physical map of area being duplicated

Background Information
The relief map should be a culminating activity after thoroughly studying an area. Students should already be familiar with the major land masses of the area you are mapping.

Management
1. Students may work on an individual map or a group map.
2. There are three stages to this activity: the forming stage, painting stage, and the labeling stage.
3. If possible, arrange to do the maps in the cafeteria or another room with tables. Cover all tables with butcher paper to ease clean-up.
4. Plan a "free-time menu" or additional activity that students will do when they are finished with their maps.
5. Place one copy of the *Recipe*, enclosed in a transparent envelope or ziplock baggie, on each table.
6. Prepare an area where the maps can dry.
7. *With parental/adult help*: Arrange for parent volunteers to work as group leaders, one for every six students. Assign students to groups. Students should bring a mixing container and two baggies, one filled with 250 ml flour and the other filled with 125 ml salt, from home. All groups can work at the same time.
8. *Without parental/adult help*: Purchase salt and flour, 10 pounds of each per class of 30. Organize the class into groups. Have one or two groups measure and mix dough while the others complete other class assignments. After mixing, they take the dough to their desk and begin the map. New groups start mixing. Repeat until everyone is done. Circulate between those mixing and those working on the maps.

THE KEY to successful relief map-making lesson is to be well organized and have everything ready in advance.

Procedure
1. Send the *Relief Note* home the day before the activity.
2. Assemble all materials and prepare the work area (see *Management*).
3. Assign students to their group and/or leader.

4. Gather in the work area. Review student behavior expectations and what students are to do when their maps are completed.

Forming Stage
5. Students should glue their outline maps onto the cardboard bases.
6. Have students mix the flour and salt in the bowls, using tongue depressors or their fingers. Add water to the mixture to form the dough.
7. Direct students to put the dough on their maps and form the major physical features of the region. Place toothpicks in the places to be labeled.
8. Have students put their maps in the designated drying area and clean up their work space.

Painting Stage
9. Students should paint their maps using an elevation color key, take them to the drying area, and clean up their work space.

Labeling Stage
10. Instruct students to label the major physical features, cities, and landmarks on their maps. Write on a gummed label or 5 cm strip of masking tape and fold it in half around the toothpick.

Discussion
1. Why do we need maps?
2. How is a relief map different from a flat map? [It is three-dimensional; you can see elevations.]
3. How does a relief map help us to understand more about an area?
4. Why do most map makers use the same colors for elevation? [for standardization]

Extension
Have students combine the primary colors to make the standard elevation colors for painting their maps.

Curriculum Correlation
Art
Have students make relief maps of their faces. Paint the maps to match the standard elevation colors.

Language Arts
Create a country from the face maps. Write a fictional report including imports, exports, flag, major features, places of interest, etc.

Relief Note!

Dear Parent,

We have been studying _____ in history. Our final activity of the unit will be the making of relief maps. Please have your child measure 250ml (1cup) flour and 125ml (½ cup) salt into two separate plastic baggies. Make sure each baggie is sealed and send to school on _____. Thank you for your support.

Sincerely,

_____

- -

Recipe

METRIC	STANDARD
250ml flour	1 cup flour
125ml salt	½ cup salt
125ml water, approximately	½ cup water, approximately

1. With your hands or a tongue depressor, mix the flour and salt in your bowl. Add a little of the water at a time until the mixture resembles play dough. You may not use all the water. DO NOT MAKE THE MIXTURE RUNNY!
2. Place the dough on your map which has been glued to cardboard and form your relief map. Use the maps in the room to guide you in placing the major physical features. Press toothpicks into each area you are going to label.
3. Put your map in the drying area. It will dry in about one week.
4. Clean up.

Topic
Contour mapping

Key Questions
1. If you were on a backpacking trip, how could you actually *see* how high you are going to climb?
2. Which mountain matches this map?

Focus
Students will draw cross sections of a contour map, double the size of the map, and construct a three-dimensional replica.

Math
NCTM Standards
  • *Make and use measurements in problems and everyday situations*
  • *Visualize and represent geometric figures with special attention to developing spatial sense*
Measurement
  volume
Ratios
Patterns
Geometry and spatial sense

Project 2061 Benchmarks
  • *Measure and mix dry and liquid materials (in the kitchen, garage, or laboratory) in prescribed amounts, exercising reasonable safety.*
  • *Geometric figures, number sequences, graphs, diagrams, sketches, number lines, maps, and stories can be used to represent objects, events, and processes in the real world, although such representations can never be exact in every detail.*

Social Science
Geography
  topography

Processes
Observing
Classifying
Comparing
Interpreting data
Applying
Working cooperatively
Communicating ideas
Making and reading maps

Materials
For each map:
  125 ml water (1/2 cup)
  125 ml salt (1/2 cup)
  250 ml flour (1 cup)
  16 cm square cardboard map base

For the class:
  metric rulers
  dinner knives
  rolling pin
  tables or other flat surfaces
  straight pins
  mixing containers such as trimmed milk cartons

Background Information
Contour or topographic maps are used to show varying elevations. The National Forest Service, National Park Service, city planners, landscapers, land developers, and hikers use them. Originally geographers mapped most of the United States using transits (surveyor's instruments for measuring horizontal angles) and levels, a time-consuming process. These men placed most benchmarks and section markers. Many mountains and other geographical points were named by and for them. Large area maps are now generally drawn using aerial photography and ground-checking.

A mountain is a part of the land that rises at least 610 m (2,000 ft.) above the surrounding area. One-fifth of the continents are covered by mountains. There are many in Asia, but few in Africa and Australia.

While it is the policy of AIMS to utilize the metric system, this activity uses foot measurements since this is the current common reference used for mountain heights.

Management
1. This activity is intended for groups of two to three. It is divided among three days. On *Day 1*, students draw cross sections and enlarge *Map A*. *Day 2* is for mixing dough and making the flour-salt maps. If space is limited, consider having part of the class build their maps each day until all are done. Leave them to dry for three or more days, depending on the weather. On *Day 3*, paint the maps.
2. See *Procedure 6* to familiarize yourself with the procedure for marking cross sections.
3. The recipe for the flour-salt mixture is: 2 parts flour, 1 part salt, and 1 part water. Add water until the dough is stiff enough to form a ball, but not sticky. It is likely you will not need all of the water. (See *Materials* for specific measures.)
4. Cover flat tables with butcher paper and sprinkle with flour before rolling dough.

Procedure

Day 1

1. Ask the first *Key Question.* Give each group one of the contour maps, two copies of the *Map A and B* sheet, and the cardboard base.
2. Each group should glue their contour map in the space labeled *Map A.* It may be glued in either direction.
3. Students should draw the grid lines marked 1 cm apart on *Map A* and 2 cm apart on *Map B.* They should also draw the grid lines on the second copy of *Map B,* cut it out, and glue it on the cardboard base.
4. Direct students to enlarge *Map A* on *Map B* (first sheet) by duplicating the line patterns, square by square.
5. Have students figure the scale for *Map B* by doubling *Map A's* scale.
6. Distribute the cross section sheet and instruct students to draw the cross sections of both maps. Find the line labeled *AB* on *Map A.* If it goes through the highest contour of the mountain, use this line to mark each elevation as shown below. If it does not cross the highest elevation, use a parallel grid line that does. It is helpful to fold along the chosen line. On the bottom line of the cross section, mark the outermost contours. Then move the map up to the 500-foot line and mark the next contour. When all the marks have been made, connect them with lines. Complete *CD, EF,* and *GH* in the same way.

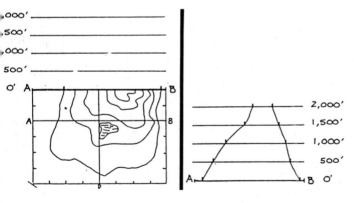

Mark each contour along the line indicated or one parallel to it (left); then connect the marks (right).

7. Compare the cross sections of the larger and smaller maps. Why are they different?

Day 2

8. Have students make the flour-salt mixture and roll or pat the dough to about a 1/2 cm thickness. They should put the remaining copy of *Map B* over the dough and puncture it with a pin along the outer contour line. Remove the paper and, with a dinner knife, cut the dough along the pin holes.
9. Students should transfer and position the dough layer on the cardboard base, matching cross sec-

tion letters and grid lines. Repeat for each contour, stacking the layers on top of each other. When the layers have been completed, pat the edges lightly to blend the mountain contours.
10. Let the maps dry.

Day 3

11. Together, study elevation maps and devise a color key for the elevations. Have students paint the map accordingly.
12. Assemble all the relief maps in one place, pick one up at a time, and ask the second *Key Question.* Have students find the matching mystery mountain. A second option is to give all the maps and mountains letter and number codes. Individuals or small groups can take turns recording matching pairs on a piece of paper.
13. Continue with other *Discussion* questions.

Discussion

1. Why are the cross sections of *Map A* and *Map B* different? [When a map is enlarged, everything appears flatter or more spread out.]
2. Which mountain matches this map? (Hold up one of the six maps.)
3. Find pairs of mountains that match.
4. Which mountain is a mesa? (has a flat top and steep sides)
5. If your mountain has a lake, what would be the most likely path of a river flowing from it?
6. When might you want to consult a contour or topographic map? [if you were building the transcontinental railroad or going on an expedition, going on a backpacking trip, finding a lost person, planning a city, etc.]

Extensions

1. Double *Map B* and draw a cross section. Compare to the cross sections of *Maps A* and *B.*
2. Bring USGS topographic maps and/or hiking books which show cross sections of trails. One such book is *Sierra South* by Thomas Winnett, published by Wilderness Press (Berkeley, CA).
3. Make up your own map and follow the same procedure.
2. Do other activities leading to the construction of topographic maps from the AIMS book, *Through the Eyes of Explorers.*

Curriculum Correlation

Art/Math/Writing

Design and mark a hiking trail to the top of your mountain. Determine the approximate length of the trail. Write about your hike. Would it be easy, moderate, or strenuous? What kind of vegetation and animal life would you see? Would you camp overnight? What would the weather be like? During what month would you go?

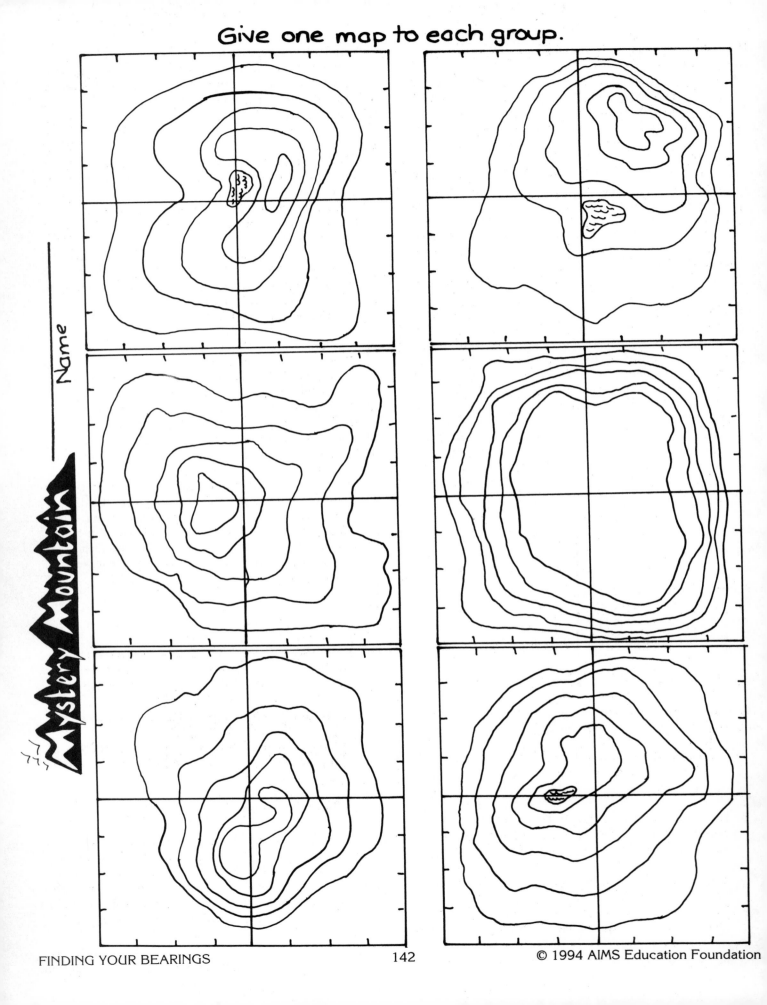

Name

Mystery Mountain

142

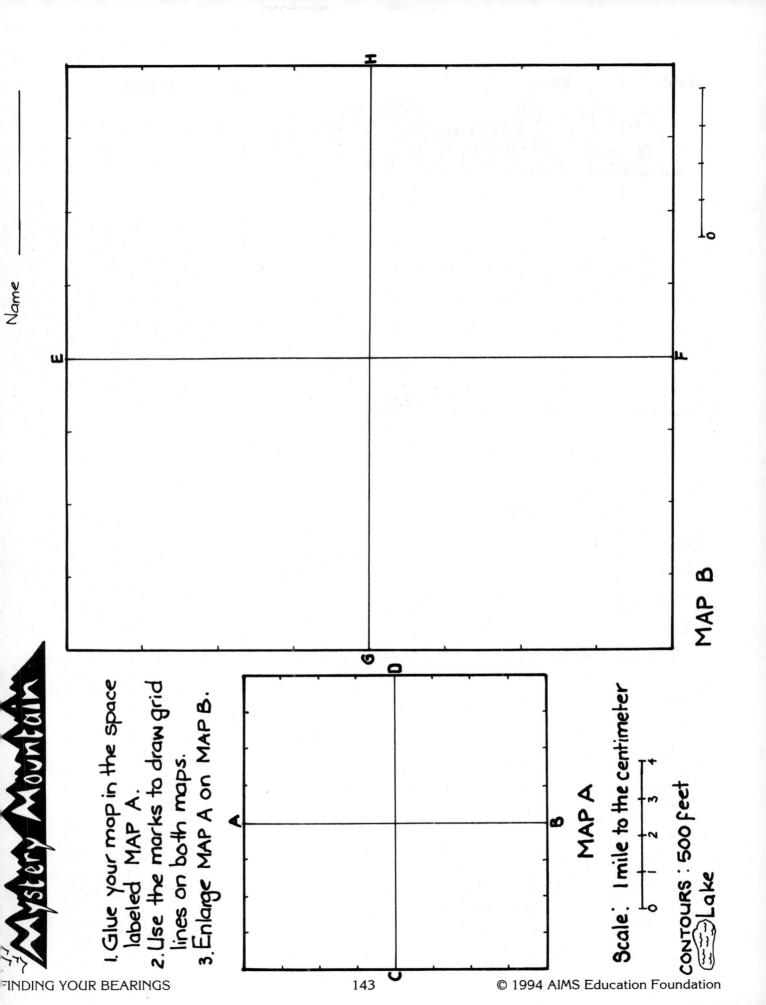

Name _____

Mystery Mountain

1. Glue your map in the space labeled MAP A.
2. Use the marks to draw grid lines on both maps.
3. Enlarge MAP A on MAP B.

MAP A

Scale: 1 mile to the centimeter

0 1 2 3 4

CONTOURS: 500 feet

Lake

MAP B

4. Construct cross sections AB and CD from Map A.

_____ 2,000´ _____
_____ 1,500´ _____
_____ 1,000´ _____
_____ 500´ _____
A _____ B 0´ C _____ D

5. Construct cross sections EF and GH from Map B and compare with cross sections AB and CD.

2,000´ _____
1,500´ _____
1,000´ _____
500´ _____
0´ E _____ F

2,000´ _____
1,500´ _____
1,000´ _____
500´ _____
0´ G _____ H

6. Build Map B with salt and flour on a 16 cm x 16 cm piece of cardboard.

144

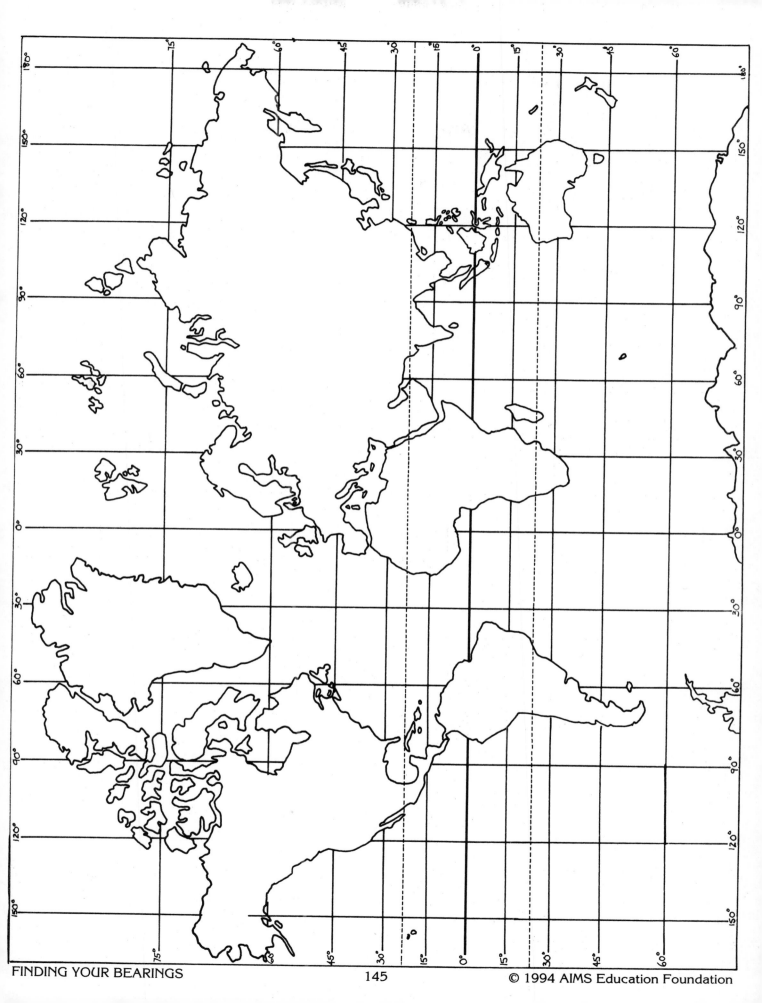

Cut along dotted lines and glue, matching the arrows at 0° longitude.

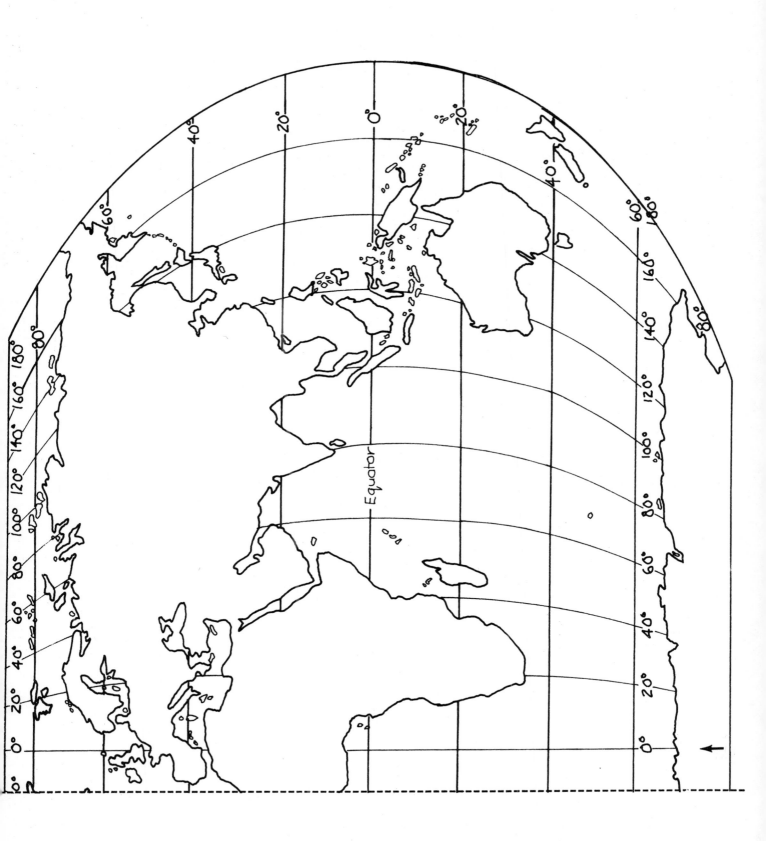

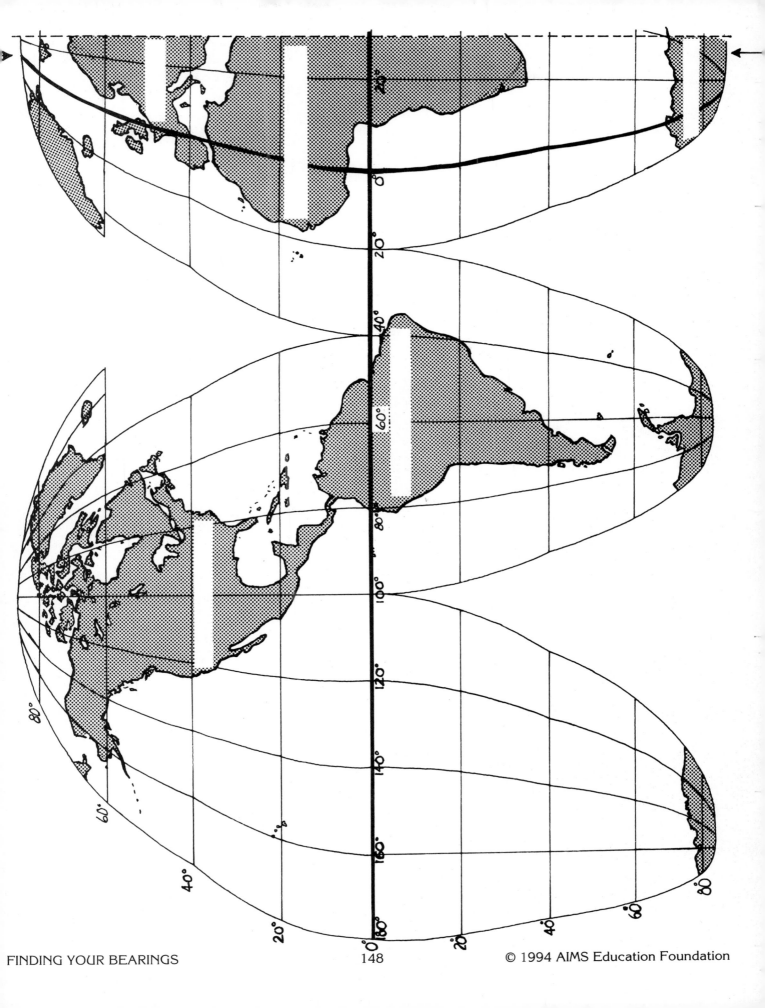

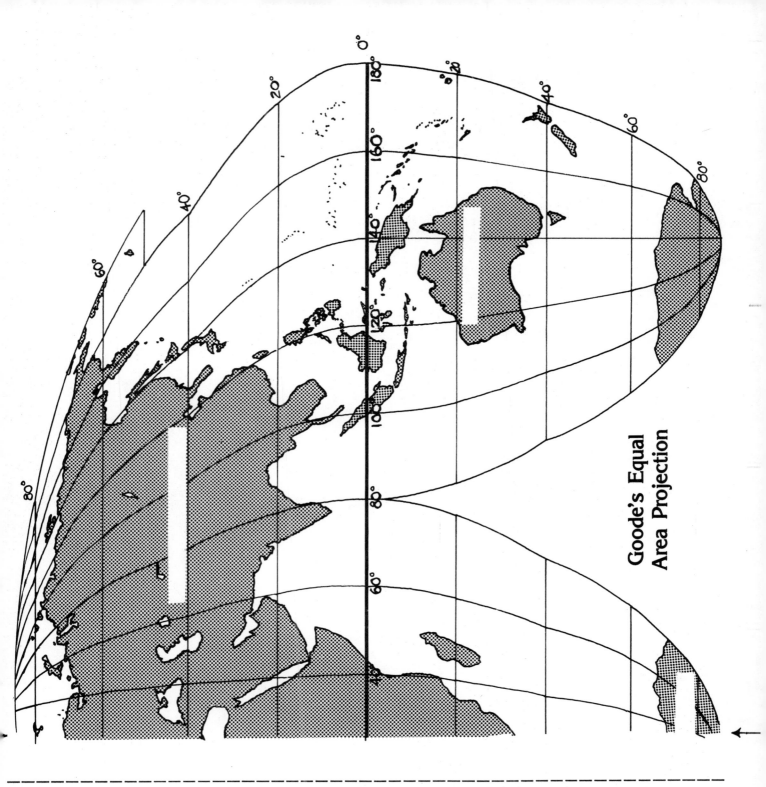

**Goode's Equal
Area Projection**

Cut along dotted line and glue flap.
Be sure that the arrows meet.

The AIMS Program

AIMS is the acronym for "Activities Integrating Mathematics and Science." Such integration enriches learning and makes it meaningful and holistic. AIMS began as a project of Fresno Pacific College to integrate the study of mathematics and science in Grades K-9, but has since expanded to include language arts, social studies, and other disciplines.

AIMS is a continuing program of the non-profit AIMS Education Foundation. It had its inception in a National Science Foundation funded program whose purpose was to explore the effectiveness of integrating mathematics and science. The project directors in cooperation with eighty elementary classroom teachers devoted two years to a thorough field-testing of the results and implications of integration.

The approach met with such positive results that the decision was made to launch a program to create instructional materials incorporating this concept. Despite the fact that thoughtful educators have long recommended an integrative approach, very little appropriate material was available in 1981 when the project began. A series of writing projects have ensued and today the AIMS Education Foundation is committed to continue the creation of new integrated activities on a permanent basis.

The AIMS program is funded through the sale of this developing series of books and proceeds from the Foundation's endowment. All net income from book and poster sales flow into a trust fund administered by the AIMS Education Foundation. Use of these funds is restricted to support of research, development, publication of new materials, and partial scholarships for classroom teachers participating in writing and field testing teams. Writers donate all their rights to the Foundation to support its on-going program. No royalties are paid to the writers.

The rationale for integration lies in the fact that science, mathematics, language arts, social studies, etc., are integrally interwoven in the real world from which it follows that they should be similarly treated in the classroom where we are preparing students to live in that world. Teachers who use the AIMS program give enthusiastic endorsement to the effectiveness of this approach.

Science encompasses the art of questioning, investigating, hypothesizing, discovering and communicating. Mathematics is the language that provides clarity, objectivity, and understanding. The language arts provide us powerful tools of communication. Many of the major contemporary societal issues stem from advancements in science and must be studied in the context of the social sciences. Therefore, it is timely that all of us take seriously a more holistic mode of educating our students. This goal motivates all who are associated with the AIMS Program. We invite you to join us in this effort.

Meaningful integration of knowledge is a major recommendation coming from the nation's professional science and mathematics associations. The American Association for the Advancement of Science in *Science for All Americans* strongly recommends the integration of mathematics, science and technology. The National Council of Teachers of Mathematics places strong emphasis on applications of mathematics such as are found in science investigations. AIMS is fully aligned with these recommendations.

Extensive field testing of AIMS investigations confirms these beneficial results.

1. Mathematics becomes more meaningful, hence more useful, when it is applied to situations that interest students.
2. The extent to which science is studied and understood is increased, with a significant economy of time, when mathematics and science are integrated.
3. There is improved quality of learning and retention, supporting the thesis that learning which is meaningful and relevant is more effective.
4. Motivation and involvement are increased dramatically as students investigate real world situations and participate actively in the process.

We invite you to become part of this classroom teacher movement by using an integrated approach to learning and sharing any suggestions you may have. The AIMS Program welcomes you!

AIMS Education Foundation Programs

A Day With AIMS

Intensive one-day workshops are offered to introduce educators to the philosophy and rationale of AIMS. Participants will discuss the methodology of AIMS and the strategies by which AIMS principles may be incorporated into curriculum. Each participant will take part in a variety of hands-on AIMS investigations to gain an understanding of such aspects as the scientific/mathematical content, classroom management, and connections with other curricular areas. The *A Day With AIMS* workshops may be offered anywhere in the United States. Necessary supplies and take-home materials are usually included in the enrollment fee.

AIMS One-Week Workshops

Throughout the nation, AIMS offers many one-week workshops each year, usually in the summer. Each workshop lasts five days and includes at least 30 hours of AIMS hands-on instruction. Participants are grouped according to the grade level(s) in which they are interested. Instructors are members of the AIMS Instructional Leadership Network. Supplies for the activities and a generous supply of take-home materials are included in the enrollment fee. Sites are selected on the basis of applications submitted by educational organizations. If chosen to host a workshop, the host agency agrees to provide specified facilities and cooperate in the promotion of the workshop. The AIMS Education Foundation supplies workshop materials as well as the travel, housing, and meals for instructors.

AIMS One-Week Fresno Pacific College Workshops

Each summer, Fresno Pacific College offers AIMS one-week workshops on the campus of Fresno Pacific College in Fresno, California. AIMS Program Directors and highly qualified members of the AIMS National Leadership Network serve as instructors.

The Science Festival and the Festival of Mathematics

Each summer, Fresno Pacific College offers a Science Festival and a Festival of Mathematics. These two-week festivals have gained national recognition as inspiring and challenging experiences, giving unique opportunities to experience hands-on mathematics and science in topical and grade level groups. Guest faculty includes some of the nation's most highly regarded mathematics and science educators. Supplies and take-home materials are included in the enrollment fee.

The AIMS Instructional Leadership Program

This is an AIMS staff development program seeking to prepare facilitators for leadership roles in science/math education in their home districts or regions. Upon successful completion of the program, trained facilitators become members of the AIMS Instructional Leadership Network, qualified to conduct AIMS workshops, teach AIMS in-service courses for college credit, and serve as AIMS consultants. Intensive training is provided in mathematics, science, processing skills, workshop management, and other relevant topics.

College Credit and Grants

Those who participate in workshops may often qualify for college credit. If the workshop takes place on the campus of Fresno Pacific College, that institution may grant appropriate credit. If the workshop takes place off-campus, arrangements can sometimes be made for credit to be granted by another college or university. In addition, the applicant's home school district is often willing to grant in-service or professional development credit. Many educators who participate in AIMS workshops are recipients of various types of educational grants, either local or national. Nationally known foundations and funding agencies have long recognized the value of AIMS mathematics and science workshops to educators. The AIMS Education Foundation encourages educators interested in attending or hosting workshops to explore the possibilities suggested above. Although the Foundation strongly supports such interest, it reminds applicants that they have the primary responsibility for fulfilling *current* requirements.

For current information regarding the programs described above, please complete the following:

Information Request

Please send current information on the items checked:

____ *Basic Information Packet* on AIMS materials
____ *Festival of Mathematics*
____ *Science Festival*
____ *AIMS Instructional Leadership Program*

____ *AIMS One-Week Fresno Pacific College Workshops*
____ *AIMS One-Week Workshops*
____ Hosting information for *A Day With AIMS* workshops
____ Hosting information for *A Week With AIMS* workshops

Name _____

Address _____
        Street   City   State   Zip

AIMS Program Publications

GRADES K-4 SERIES
Bats Incredible
Brinca de Alegria Hacia la Primavera con las Matemáticas y Ciencias
Cáete de Gusto Hacia el Otoño con la Matemáticas y Ciencias
Fall Into Math and Science
Glide Into Winter With Math and Science
Hardhatting in a Geo-World
Jawbreakers and Heart Thumpers
Overhead and Underfoot
Patine al Invierno con Matemáticas y Ciencias
Popping With Power
Primariamente Física
Primariamente Plantas
Primarily Physics
Primarily Plants
Sense-able Science
Spring Into Math and Science

GRADES K-6 SERIES
Budding Botanist
Critters
Mostly Magnets
Principalmente Imanes
Ositos Nada Más
Primarily Bears
Water Precious Water

GRADES 5-9 SERIES
Down to Earth
Electrical Connections
Finding Your Bearings (Revised Edition)
Floaters and Sinkers
From Head to Toe
Fun With Foods
Historical Connections in Mathematics, Volume I
Historical Connections in Mathematics, Volume II
Machine Shop
Math + Science, A Solution
Our Wonderful World
Out of This World (Revised Edition)
Pieces and Patterns, A Patchwork in Math and Science
Piezas y Diseños, un Mosaic de Matemáticas y Ciencias
Soap Films and Bubbles
The Sky's the Limit (Revised Edition)

FOR FURTHER INFORMATION WRITE TO:

AIMS Education Foundation • P.O. Box 8120 • Fresno, California 93747-8120

We invite you to subscribe to $\mathcal{AIMS}$!

Each issue of $\mathcal{AIMS}$ contains a variety of material useful to educators at all grade levels. Feature articles of lasting value deal with topics such as mathematical or science concepts, curriculum, assessment, the teaching of processing skills, and historical background. Several of the latest AIMS math/science investigations are always included, along with their reproducible activity sheets. As needs direct and space allows, various issues contain news of current developments, such as workshop schedules, activities of the AIMS Instructional Leadership Network, and announcements of upcoming publications.

$\mathcal{AIMS}$ is published monthly, August through May. Subscriptions are on an annual basis only. A subscription entered at any time will begin with the next issue, but will also include the previous issues of that volume. Readers have preferred this arrangement because articles and activities within an annual volume are often interrelated.

Please note that an $\mathcal{AIMS}$ subscription automatically includes duplication rights for one school site for all issues included in the subscription. Many schools build cost-effective library resources with their subscriptions.

YES! I am interested in subscribing to $\mathcal{AIMS}$.

Name _____   Home Phone _____

Address _____   City, State, Zip _____

Please send the following volumes (subject to availability):

_____ Volume I (1986-87) $27.50	_____ Volume VI (1991-92) $27.50
_____ Volume II (1987-88) $27.50	_____ Volume VII (1992-93) $27.50
_____ Volume III (1988-89) $27.50	_____ Volume VIII (1993-94) $27.50
_____ Volume IV (1989-90) $27.50	_____ Volume IX (1994-95) $27.50
_____ Volume V (1990-91) $27.50	

_____ Limited offer: Volumes IX & X (1994-95 & 1996-97) $50.00

(Note: Prices may change without notice. For current prices, call (209) 255-4094.)

Check your method of payment:

☐ Check enclosed in the amount of $ _____

☐ Purchase order attached (Please be sure it includes the P.O. number, the authorizing signature, and the position of the authorizing person.)

☐ Credit Card   (Check One)
    ☐ Visa   ☐ MasterCard   Number _____

Amount $ _____   Expiration Date _____

Signature _____   Today's Date_____

Make checks payable to **AIMS Education Foundation.**
Mail to $\mathcal{AIMS}$ *Magazine*, P.O. Box 8120, Fresno, CA 93747-8120.

AIMS Duplication Rights Program

AIMS has received many requests from school districts for the purchase of unlimited duplication rights to AIMS materials. In response, the AIMS Education Foundation has formulated the program outlined below. There is a built-in flexibility which, we trust, will provide for those who use AIMS materials extensively to purchase such rights for either individual activities or entire books.

It is the goal of the AIMS Education Foundation to make its materials and programs available at reasonable cost. All income from sale of publications and duplication rights is used to support AIMS programs. Hence, strict adherence to regulations governing duplication is essential. Duplication of AIMS materials beyond limits set by copyright laws and those specified below is strictly forbidden.

Limited Duplication Rights

Any purchaser of an AIMS book may make up to *200 copies* of any activity in that book for use at *one school site*. Beyond that, rights must be purchased according to the appropriate category.

Unlimited Duplication Rights for Single Activities

An individual or school may purchase the right to make an unlimited number of copies of a single activity. The royalty is $5.00 per activity per school site.

Examples: 3 activities x 1 site x $5.00 = $15.00
          9 activities x 3 sites x $5.00 = $135.00

Unlimited Duplication Rights for Whole Books

A school or district may purchase the right to make an unlimited number of copies of a single, *specified* book. The royalty is $20.00 per book per school site. This is in addition to the cost of the book.

Examples: 5 books x 1 site x $20.00 = $100.00
          12 books x 10 sites x $20.00 = $2400.00

Magazine/Newsletter Duplication Rights

Members of the AIMS Education Foundation who Purchase the *AIMS* Magazine/Newsletter are hereby granted permission to make up to 200 copies of any portion of it, provided these copies will be used for educational purposes.

Workshop Instructors' Duplication Rights

Workshop instructors may distribute to registered workshop participants: a maximum of 100 copies of any article and /or 100 copies of no more than 8 activities, provided these 6 conditions are met:

1. Since all AIMS activities are based upon the *AIMS Model of Mathematics* and the *AIMS Model of Learning*, leaders must include in their presentations an explanation of these two models.
2. Workshop instructors must relate the AIMS activities presented to these basic explanations of the AIMS philosophy of education.
3. The copyright notice must appear on all materials distributed.
4. Instructors must provide information enabling participants to apply for membership in the AIMS Education Foundation or order books from the Foundation.
5. Instructors must inform participants of their limited duplication rights as outlined below.
6. Only student pages may be duplicated.

Written permission must be obtained for duplication beyond the limits listed above. Additional royalty payments may be required.

Workshop Participants' Rights

Those enrolled in workshops in which AIMS student activity sheets are distributed may duplicate a maximum of 35 copies or enough to use the lessons one time with one class, whichever is less. Beyond that, rights must be purchased according to the appropriate category.

Application for Duplication Rights

The purchasing agency or individual must clearly specify the following:
1. Name, address, and telephone number
2. Titles of the books for Unlimited Duplication Rights contracts
3. Titles of activities for Unlimited Duplication Rights contracts
4. Names and addresses of school sites for which duplication rights are being purchased

NOTE: Books to be duplicated must be purchased separately and are not included in the contract for Unlimited Duplication Rights.

The requested duplication rights are automatically authorized when proper payment is received, although a *Certificate of Duplication Rights* will be issued when the application is processed.

Address all correspondence to
> **Contract Division**
> **AIMS Education Foundation**
> **P.O. Box 8120**
> **Fresno, CA 93747-8120**